Plas Newydd

Isle of Anglesey

George Charles Henry Victor,
Marquis of Anglesey

THE NATIONAL TRUST

2009

Plas Newydd lies one mile south-west of Llanfairpwll and the A5
(and about two miles from the Menai Bridge) on the A4080.

Acknowledgements

The section on the Griffith, Bayly and Paget families and part of that on
the garden are written by the Marquess of Anglesey, to whom the Trust
is also greatly indebted for much of the information in the rest of this
guidebook. Thanks are also due to Mr John Cornforth, Mr H. M. Colvin,
Dr Frances Fergusson, Mr A. Giles Jones, Archivist at the University
College of North Wales, Mr David Jenkins, of the National Library of
Wales, and Dr John Martin Robinson.

GERVASE JACKSON-STOPS, 1976

For this edition Lord Anglesey has revised and extended his essay on the
family history, and we are further indebted to him. Alastair Laing, the
Trust's Adviser on Paintings and Sculpture, has revised the descriptions
of the paintings, and additional information has been drawn from the
Plas Newydd MSS at the University College of North Wales. The Trust is
grateful to the Archivist, Mr Tomos Roberts, for his usual helpfulness.
The Trust is also grateful to Mr Jonathan Harris for the comments
and suggestions he has supplied, and to Sir Oliver Millar, Dr Frederick van
Kretschmar, Dr Malcolm Rogers, Mrs Margaret Hughes,
Mr J. A. Reeves, Mr John Underwood and Mr Arthur Trevor.

JONATHAN MARSDEN, 1992

(*Cover*) King Neptune's crown and trident rest against an urn and his wet footprints can still be seen on the flagstones, as if he had just risen from the sea to join
the family at table; detail from Rex Whistler's mural in the Rex Whistler Room

(*Title-page*) Design drawn in 1936 by Rex Whistler for a bookplate for the Earl of
Uxbridge, later 7th and present Marquess of Anglesey

Photographs: Country Life page 25; Country Life/Alex Starkey pages 5, 7
(above), 11, 24, 31, 33, 54; Courtauld Institute of Art pages 12, 13, 21, 60, 62, 63, 65,
70 (left); John Mills Photography Ltd pages 1, 16, 45, 67; Molyneux Photography
page 17; National Library of Wales page 9; National Trust pages 7 (below), 37, 39,
47, 49, 51, 59, 69; NT/John Hammond front cover, pages 41, 46, 68;
National Trust Photographic Library/Andreas von Einsiedel page 70 (right);
Sir John Soane's Museum page 55; Archifau a Chagliadau Arbennig, Prifysgol
Bangor/Archives and Special Collections, Bangor University page 53 (above
and below).

Contents

Plas Newydd

Plas Newydd* belonged from about 1470 to the powerful Griffith family of Penrhyn, who built the original hall-house here early in the following century, and from whom the estate descended by marriage to the Bagenal and Bayly families. Between 1751 and 1753 Sir Nicholas Bayly, Bt, added to this building a semicircular turret in the middle of the east front (facing the Menai Strait), and an octagonal tower at the south-east corner. It was these two additions in the Gothick taste which dictated both the style and unusual plan of the present house, completed by his successor.

Sir Nicholas's son, Henry, inherited through his mother the title of Lord Paget of Beaudesert and in 1784, two years after inheriting Plas Newydd, was created Earl of Uxbridge. His alterations to the house were undertaken in two distinct stages: the first in 1783–6, when John Cooper of Beaumaris built a second octagonal tower at the northern end of the east front to make it symmetrical, and when the rooms behind this façade were substantially remodelled; the second (enabled by increased revenues from copper mining on Anglesey and coal in Staffordshire) in 1793–9, when James Wyatt and Joseph Potter of Lichfield between them formed a new entrance front on the west, created all the Neo-classical and Gothick interiors of the present main block, and built the Stables (also in the Gothick style) to the north-west of the house. Potter added the north wing with an elaborate chapel on the first floor between 1805 and 1809, and continued to be employed on farm buildings and lesser alterations to the house into the 1820s, while Humphry Repton was consulted on the layout of the park and gardens, producing one of his famous 'Red Books' for Plas Newydd in 1799.

In 1812 the estate passed to Lord Uxbridge's eldest son, Henry William, three years later created 1st Marquess of Anglesey for his heroism at Waterloo, where he lost a leg. Lord Anglesey lived chiefly at Beaudesert in Staffordshire, while Plas Newydd was either closed down or let for long periods. Apart from the conversion of the chapel into a private theatre by the 5th Marquess about 1900, no major changes were made to the house until the 1930s, when the 6th Marquess, with H. S. Goodhart-Rendel as his architect, removed the battlements from the parapets around the house, shortened the two tall pinnacles on the east front (giving them Tudor caps to match those on the entrance side), and altered the form of all the sash-windows. At the same time he entirely remodelled the north wing, destroying the chapel-theatre, but creating

---

* Plas Newydd means 'New Place' or 'New Mansion'. At what time the house first acquired the name is not certain, but it was so called as early as the last three decades of the fifteenth century. In the 1750s Sir Nicholas Bayly was addressing letters to and from 'Placenewith', but this seems to have been an idiosyncrasy rather than an accepted English alternative.

on the ground floor a long dining-room, decorated by Rex Whistler between 1936 and 1940 with what many regard as his masterpiece in *trompe-l'œil* painting. Also in the 1930s, much of the house interior was redecorated by Sybil Colefax, and a substantial quantity of furniture was introduced to Plas Newydd from Beaudesert, which was demolished in 1935.

In 1976 Plas Newydd was given to the National Trust by the 7th Marquess of Anglesey, together with 169 acres of garden, park and woodland, including a mile and a half of coastline along the Menai Strait. Lord and Lady Anglesey still live in part of the house, while the Stables and many of the outbuildings (formerly occupied by the HMS *Conway* Training School) continue to be leased by Cheshire County Council for educational purposes and outdoor activities. These areas of Plas Newydd, which include the neolithic cromlech in front of the Stables, are not open to the public.

The Approach to the House

From the Anglesey end of the Britannia Bridge, the short journey to Plas Newydd via the village normally abbreviated as 'Llanfair P.G.' takes in several objects of relevance to the house and its family which lie outside the property of the National Trust. Most prominent is the commemorative column erected by subscription in 1817 in honour of the 1st Marquess of Anglesey, the great cavalry commander at Waterloo, and designed by Thomas Harrison of Chester. The bronze figure of the Marquess at the top, by Matthew Noble, was added in 1860, six years after his death (see p. 67).

At the water's edge by St Mary's church below the column is a colossal figure of another hero of that time – Lord Nelson, carved and erected as a marker for shipping by one of Lord Anglesey's sons, Lord Clarence Paget, in the 1850s. He was a keen sailor and, as Secretary to the Navy, founded the Naval Reserve Force.

A short distance along the road that forks left at the best-preserved tollhouse on Thomas Telford's Holyhead Road is the Grand Lodge to Plas Newydd, with an arch-screen designed by Joseph Potter around 1805. Visitors today enter the grounds near the second lodge approximately one mile along the park wall.

The Dairy

The visitors' car-park lies beside the early nineteenth-century Dairy, a low building with Gothick lattice windows, and with a tiled milking parlour (now the tea-room) in the centre, crowned by two air vents in the form of miniature castellated cupolas. Designs for an octagonal dairy made about 1794 by Joseph Potter, James Wyatt's collaborator at Plas Newydd, appear not to have been executed, but this building may represent an alternative scheme by Potter of around 1810, when he altered the farm and cottages on the estate. The National Trust has converted the Dairy buildings to accommodate a shop and lavatories for visitors as well as the tea-room.

The Stables*

From the front of the Dairy, across a wide lawn, can be seen the turreted and castellated façade of the Stable block. This was built by Potter in 1797, possibly based on an initial idea by James Wyatt, to whose early work in the Gothick manner (such as Sandleford Priory in Berkshire, and Sheffield Park in East Sussex, another National

* Please note that there is no access to the Stable block or the cromlech.

6

(*Above*) The Stables

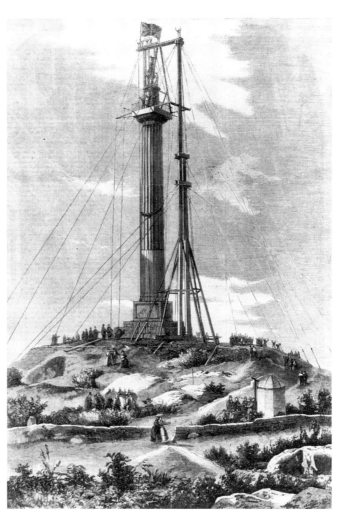

(*Right*) The raising of the
Anglesey statue, from
The Illustrated London News,
15 December 1860

Trust property) it bears a marked resemblance. Intended for the accommodation of fourteen horses with a coach-house for two carriages, the work was supervised by Lt-Col William Peacocke, Lord Uxbridge's friend and immediate neighbour at Plas Llanfair to the north, who had also been in charge of early landscape improvements at Plas Newydd. The original stables were attached to the north side of the house, and were demolished to make way for Potter's new courtyard of kitchens and domestic offices, erected between 1799 and 1809.

In the 1740s Sir Nicholas Bayly had been the first to keep a coach on Anglesey, and its first journeys caused exceptional interest: 'the plough was deserted, the wheel stood still, and the spade was thrown down, until curiosity had been gratified by sight, or still more by the touch, of the massive fabric'.* The older-established Williams-Bulkeley family of Baron Hill was the first to have a motor car on the island (Lord Anglesey's was the second to be registered).

The Cromlech

Immediately to the right of the Stables a gap in the trees gives an incomparable view across the Strait to the mountains of Snowdonia, while to the left can be seen the cromlech. One of the best preserved of Anglesey's many neolithic monuments, this consists of four or five large boulders which once enclosed the burial chamber of one of the seafaring invaders who colonised the island long before the Roman invasion.

To the antiquarians of the eighteenth century this and other cromlechs were concrete evidence of a continuity which linked the Welsh Bards with the ancient Druids (whose last-ditch defence against the Romans is said to have taken place on the shores of the Menai) and beyond, to Hebrew scripture. Cromlechs were thought to have been built as sacrificial altars, and the priest of the local parish, Henry Rowlands, whose *Mona Antiqua Restaurata* of 1723 put this case at length and with great conviction, cited Exodus xx ('Thou shalt not build an altar of hewn stones') to explain why the upper slabs were formed of boulders and not dressed stones.

The Rev. William Bingley, writing in 1800, thought it unlikely 'that these erections should have been intended as altars for druidic sacrifices . . . The upper stones are, in general, too small, and much too high for a fire to be kindled upon them, sufficient to consume the victim, without burning the officiating priest'.

Originally the stones of the Plas Newydd cromlech would have been covered with an overburden of earth and without it they have been subject to both weather and vandalism: in 1799 Humphry Repton proposed the insertion of a 'wedge of marble' (not 'a common wedge', which 'might mislead future antiquaries'); it was to be inscribed 'To preserve A Druidical Monument which is of a date before the Christian Era (Tho' lately endangered by wanton mischief) . . .'

* Edmund Hyde Hall, *Description of Caernarvonshire*, 1809–11, quoting an 'aged informant'.

The Cromlech; by Moses Griffith (National Library of Wales)

Also within the park are the remains of a megalithic chamfered cairn or *carnedd*, and this too suffered damage in the eighteenth century, when 'Sir Henry Bayly, supposing this mound a mere heap of rubbish, began to level it, but meeting with human bones the workmen were ordered to desist.'*

The Setting

To the right of the Dairy a path leads along the edge of the wood and across the main drive to approach the house on the central axis of the west front. Much of the planting, including some large beeches, dates from just after 1798, the year in which Humphry Repton was commissioned by the Earl of Uxbridge to advise on the layout at Plas Newydd. Repton's 'Red Book' of proposals is now in the National Library of Wales, and although it now lacks its original watercolour illustrations, it is clear that a great many of the suggestions made in it were promptly adopted. One instance is the wood between the stable block and the house: originally both buildings could be seen at once from the lawn in front of the Dairy and 'the comparative magnitude & elevated station of the stables', in Repton's words, made 'the mansion, which ought, on its first appearance to be unrivalled, appear depressed & insignificant'. An easy answer to this was to bring forward 'the skreen of plantation which surrounds the offices . . . that no part of the house shd be visible from the approach'.

The magnificent position of Plas Newydd is immediately apparent from the point

* *Nicholson's Cambrian Traveller's Guide*, 1808, p. 1069.

where the path emerges on to the main drive, on a level with the roofline of the house. Above and beyond it can be seen the mountains of Snowdonia, including Snowdon itself, and immediately to the right the lawn sloping steeply to the battlemented terrace along the edge of the Strait, the shimmering water, and the woods of Vaynol on the opposite shore.

Before entering the Gothick Hall, the visitor may care to walk round to the other side of the house to see the full extent of the view along the Menai Strait in both directions. Southwards it stretches as far as the slate port of Port Dinorwic, with the mountains as a backdrop, and northwards towards the Britannia Bridge, Robert Stephenson's great masterpiece of railway engineering begun in 1845 and finished in 1850. Tragically damaged by fire in 1970, the bridge has since been rebuilt with conventional steel arches between the towers in place of the original ultra-modern tubular tunnels which used to carry the Holyhead railway. A new road deck was added in the 1970s to relieve the pressure of traffic on Telford's Menai Bridge.

In 1985, with the generous support of the National Heritage Memorial Fund and its own Enterprise Neptune appeal, the National Trust was able to purchase the coastal part of the Vaynol estate between Port Dinorwic and the Britannia Bridge, ensuring the preservation of the view from Plas Newydd, and enabling access for walkers on the opposite side of the Strait. Connections between the opposing banks go back further. In 1845 Thomas Assheton Smith of Vaynol took a lease of Plas Newydd from the 1st Marquess of Anglesey, who was living in Staffordshire. He did not renew the lease when its seven-year term came up, saying that his wife was never healthy on this side of the water. Later Sir Michael Duff, Bt, of Vaynol, married Lady Caroline Paget, a sister of the present Marquess

The Entrance Front

The main block of the house on this, the west, side is punctuated by four thin octagonal turrets rising the whole height of the building, and finishing in Tudor caps with green copper weather-vanes. Dominated in the centre by the three tall Gothic windows of the Music Room (whose ceiling comes half way up the second-floor windows above them), the symmetry of the west front, as built by Joseph Potter and James Wyatt between 1797 and 1799, has been somewhat impaired by the screen wall at right angles to the façade, designed by Rex Whistler and built in the 1930s. This was intended to provide a more sheltered main entrance, and a more inconspicuous car-park, hidden from the rest of the garden. Originally, a second porch, matching the present one, existed immediately to the left of the Music Room windows, while the three bays immediately left of the main block were set back far more deeply, thus separating it more effectively from the office wing to the north. Another alteration made by the 6th Marquess in the 1930s was to replace the original castellations round the top of the house by a plain parapet. The low conservatory is a more recent addition.

In its original, totally symmetrical, form the west front therefore presented two alternative main entrances, through identical porches, based on a 'Modell of the Portico' fashioned by the joiner in September 1797. That on the right led into the Gothick Hall (probably intended as the usual approach, then as now); that on the left emerged into the Staircase Hall, in the dark space under the middle flight of stairs. This rather odd arrangement was forced on Potter and Wyatt (if the latter was concerned with this front) by the site of the sixteenth-century Great Hall, which they simply widened at this date to form the present Music Room. Lord Uxbridge evidently wished this vast interior to be a dining-room rather than an entrance hall, making a central front door impossible: hence the expedient of the two porches, all in the cause of symmetry. Apart from the loss of the battlements, Repton, writing in 1799, found this side of the house too symmetrical – 'defective in that irregularity of outline, which is so well preserved, in the stables, & which constitutes one great beauty in Gothick architecture, & makes it so proper for those situations where the top of the house is more seen than the lower storey'.

The entrance front in 1939; by Rex Whistler (unfinished). The artist appears in the foreground, with the present Marquess riding a bicycle on the path below (Rex Whistler Exhibition)

The South and East Fronts

In 1783, immediately after Lord Uxbridge inherited Plas Newydd, a mason-architect of Beaumaris called John Cooper (who had rebuilt nearby Bodorgan Hall for the Meyricks in 1779 and was later to work at Chirk Castle) proposed the building of a second octagonal tower at the south-west corner of the house to balance the south-east tower, built by the Earl's father, Sir Nicholas Bayly, in 1753. But in the end it was considered more important to make the east rather than the south front symmetrical. Thus between 1783 and 1785 Cooper built the north-east tower containing the Billiard Room (now the Rex Whistler Exhibition) on the ground floor, and raised the roof of this side of the house, completing the façade roughly as it appears today, with a semicircular bay in the centre (Sir Nicholas's round tower of 1751) flanked by two canted bays at either end. All give splendid seaward views.

Until about 1935, the parapet along the east front was battlemented. The small octagonal turrets flanking the central bay window were far taller and terminated in small spires rather than in Tudor caps like those on the entrance front, while the windows were more conventional Georgian sashes of three by four panes. The 6th Marquess's alterations toned down the Gothick effect of the façade, but even more his remodelling and heightening of the north wing, to the right, prejudiced its symmetry. In place of the three Gothick windows of the Chapel, he substituted windows identical with those of the rest of the east front, thereby elongating the whole composition. If this change was in some ways regrettable, at the same time it made Plas Newydd

The east front in 1776; by Moses Griffith

The east front, *c*.1800; by John 'Warwick' Smith (Middle Landing)

one of the most comfortable country houses in Britain, with nearly half the bedrooms in the main block converted into bathrooms, and further guest rooms created in the wing. More important, the creation of the Rex Whistler Room inside the north wing perhaps outweighed any loss on the architectural side.

Below the east front, the battlemented sea wall and terrace was built, probably to Wyatt and Potter's designs, about 1796, when Lord Uxbridge paid a bill for 'Blasting Rock in Boathouse & Bath'. It consists of three semicircular bastions, the central one with a flagstaff (from which Lord Anglesey's banner flies during the summer) and two rectangular projections between, with open Gothick arches, one containing two rooms with fireplaces either side of a jetty stretching out in front of it, the other consisting of a small covered dock. It is possible that as well as being a boathouse, this was intended as a marine 'plunge bath'. Stationed along the walk are five 'trunnion' carronades of *c*.1830–45, from the famous Fort Belan battery across the Strait and to the south; they came as a wedding present to Lord and Lady Anglesey from Lord Newborough in 1948. Beyond the plunge bath, to the south, can be seen the small private harbour built in the 1790s, which is now used by Cheshire County Council for outward-bound courses and is not open to the public.

Plans of the House

Shaded areas not open to the public

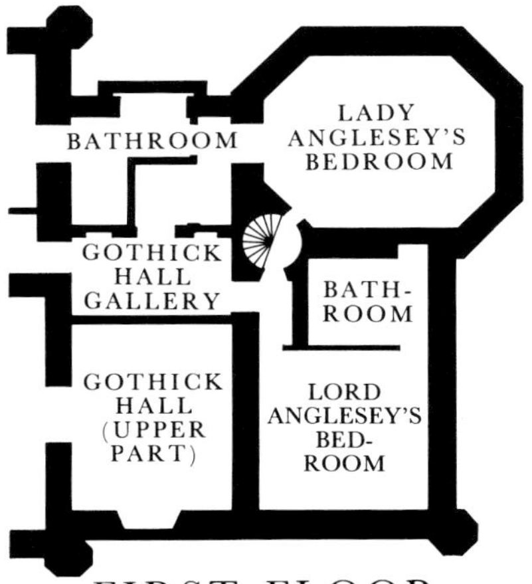

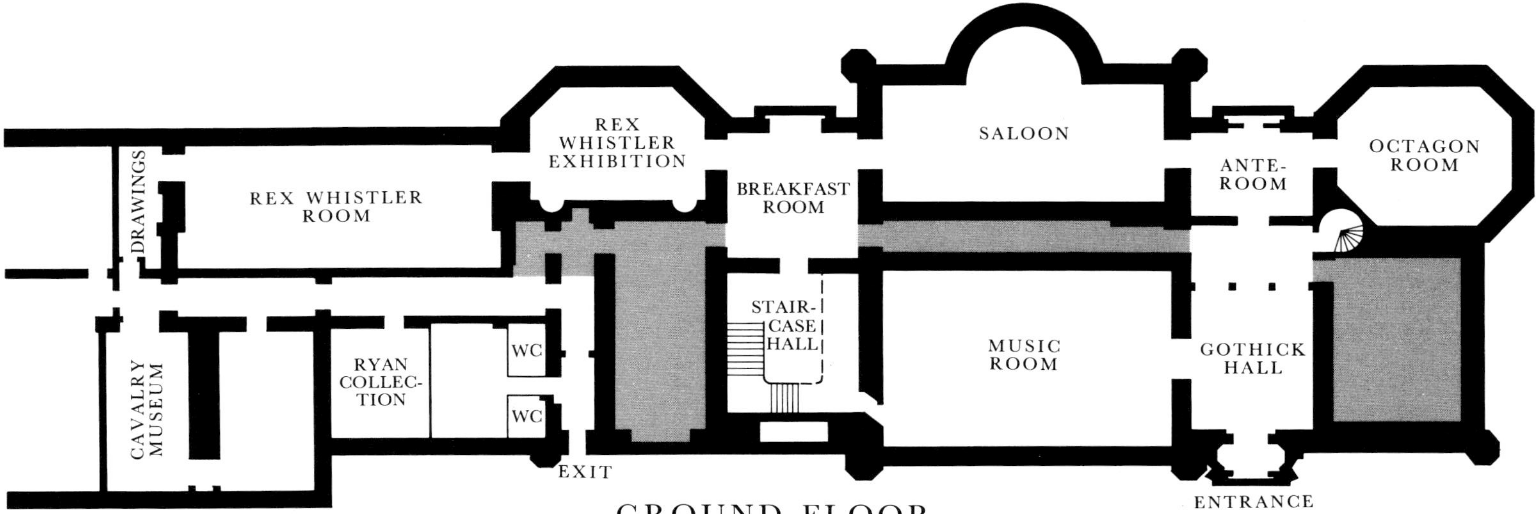

FIRST FLOOR

LADY ANGLESEY'S BEDROOM

BATHROOM

BATH-ROOM

GOTHICK HALL GALLERY

LORD ANGLESEY'S BED-ROOM

GOTHICK HALL (UPPER PART)

GROUND FLOOR

N

OCTAGON ROOM

ANTE-ROOM

GOTHICK HALL

ENTRANCE

SALOON

MUSIC ROOM

BREAKFAST ROOM

STAIR-CASE HALL

REX WHISTLER EXHIBITION

EXIT

WC

WC

RYAN COLLEC-TION

REX WHISTLER ROOM

DRAWINGS

CAVALRY MUSEUM

Tour of the House

The Gothick Hall

Originally known simply as the 'Vestibule', this high rectangular room rising through two storeys with a gallery at one end and an elaborate plaster 'fan-vault' is one of the finest late eighteenth-century interiors surviving in James Wyatt's 'Gothick' style, comparable with some of his later work at Fonthill in Wiltshire (now gone) and Ashridge in Hertfordshire. However, if Wyatt had anything to do with the decoration, it can only have been by way of preliminary ideas or advice to his collaborator, Joseph Potter of Lichfield, who signed a number of designs for the room, some of which survive at Plas Newydd (see p. 48). None of the drawings is dated, but accounts reveal that the joiners were completing their work here and in the adjoining Music Room in the spring of 1797.

Early visitors found it surprising: '. . . we, for a short time, imagined ourselves in the chapel, a mistake . . . to which every visitor is liable; the ceiling having gothic arches, with a gallery suitable to it, and several niches cut in the side walls.'* Two large niches with pinnacled canopies originally flanked the door to the Music Room, with another pair on the opposite wall. Unusually, these were recorded in 1803 as each containing 'a Crystaline Alum Pyramidical ornament'.† These niches were filled in early this century, as was the tracery of the central compartment in the vault, which was described as 'a flat lanthorn dome'.

The only other significant change to the room has been the coating of the walls and carved wooden screens with a textured paint scored with white lines to resemble stonework. The electric light-switches here and throughout the house are cast in the form of the 6th Marquess's coat of arms in brass. (*Please do not touch the switches.*)

Paintings

ENTRANCE WALL:

LEFT OF DOOR, ABOVE:

ENOCH SEEMAN (1690?-1745)

Caroline Paget, Lady Bayly (d. 1766)

Daughter and heir of Brig.-Gen. Thomas Paget, she married Sir Nicholas Bayly, 2nd Bt, in 1737 (see p. 62).

BELOW:

Manner of Sir GODFREY KNELLER, Bt (1646/9-1723), *c.*1690

Unknown Lady in mourning, wearing a fontange

* *The Cambrian Tourist, or Post-chaise Companion*, 1828, p. 179.

† Plas Newydd MSS, vi, 576. These mineralogical curiosities may have come from Lord Uxbridge's own workings at Parys Mountain.

The Gothick Hall in 1896, showing the Gothick canopied niches (now gone)

RIGHT OF DOOR, ABOVE:

ANGLO-DUTCH, late seventeenth-century

Henry, 7th Baron Paget, 1st Earl of Uxbridge (1st creation) (c.1663–1743)

A Tory politician, in May 1714 appointed Envoy Extraordinary to the Elector of Hanover (the future George I), who made him an earl.

BELOW:

HENRY MORLAND (fl. 1675–c.1708)

Sir Brownlow Sherard, 3rd Bt (1667/8–1735/6)

Gentleman-Usher of the Privy Chamber, from William III to George II. Brother of Alice Sherard, who married Sir John Brownlow, Bt, of Belton. His niece married Brigadier-General Thomas Paget.

LEFT WALL:

? Circle of FRANS SNYDERS (1579–1657)

A Bear Hunt

Possibly from the studio of Paul de Vos (1596–1678).

? After Sir ANTHONY VAN DYCK (1599–1641)

Henry Rich, 1st Earl of Holland (1590–1649), 1640

Probably painted as General of the Horse in the 1st Scottish War (1639). More courtier than commander, and a weathercock in the Civil War. Beheaded 1649. His daughter married the 5th Baron Paget.

The Gothick Hall

Sir ANTHONY VAN DYCK (1599–1641)

Unknown Lady

Now thought to represent Katherine Manners, Duchess of Buckingham (d. 1649), in her widow-hood.

The pictures above and below the balcony are seen subsequently and described on pp. 28 and 34.

RIGHT WALL:

FRANS SNYDERS (1579–1657)

A Butcher's Stall

Snyders specialised in this kind of composition, often having the figures painted by another hand; here, however, he possibly includes a self-portrait.

ENGLISH, ? eighteenth-century

William Paget, 1st Baron Paget de Beaudesert, KG (1505/6–63)

Henry VIII's chief secretary, diplomat and confidant, 'Protector' Somerset's right-hand man, and Queen Mary's Lord Privy Seal. The founder of the Paget family fortunes (see p. 58).

? FLEMISH, sixteenth-century

William Paget, 1st Baron Paget de Beaudesert, KG (1505/6–63)

Panel

The original of the three versions here, probably painted on an embassy to Philip II in Brussels in 1556. He wears the greater George (the Garter jewel).

? ENGLISH, sixteenth-century

William Paget, 1st Baron Paget de Beaudesert, KG (1505/6–63)

Panel

A variant copy of the previous picture. He wears the lesser George, half concealed. The reason for this still needs explaining.

Furniture

The set of twenty mahogany hall chairs with dished seats is painted with the arms of Paget quartering Bayly, surmounted by a baron's coronet. The chairs were made for Henry Bayly, 9th Baron, between 1769, when he succeeded to the barony, and 1784, when the earldom of Uxbridge was revived for him. Like many of the paintings and much of the furniture now at Plas Newydd, they were at Beaudesert in Staffordshire until Plas Newydd became the family's principal seat in the 1930s.

The giltwood chandeliers in the eighteenth-century style also came from Beaudesert.

Clocks and barometer

The eight-day bracket clock on the side-table is by John Pickett of Marlborough, *c.*1790.

The fourteen-day bracket clock under the balcony is by Barillet, Paris, *c.*1770. Both the clock case and the bracket are veneered in colourless horn backed by a green pigment painted with flowers. It is rare for such decoration to survive.

The barometer in the porch is by Rivolta.

Sculpture

The two small eighteenth-century alabaster busts on the side-table represent Petrarch and Dante.

Beneath the table is a marble wine-cooler, *c.*1730, with early nineteenth-century bronze feet, purchased by the 6th Marquess for the garden, but recently brought inside to preserve it from the frost.

Banners

The two crimson silk banners of the Royal Horse Guards, with silver embroidery, are early Victorian and commemorate the Peninsular and Waterloo campaigns.

The Music Room

By far the largest and most splendid room in the house, the Music Room was created at the same time as the Gothick Hall, about 1796–8, and there are designs by Potter for the treatment of each wall (see p. 48). However, the room closely resembles James Wyatt's design for the chapel at Magdalen College, Oxford, made in 1792, and for the Great Room at Auckland Castle, Co. Durham, of 1795, and so the original concept was probably also his.

The Music Room occupies much the same site as the great hall of the original sixteenth-century house of the Griffiths and Baylys (illustrated p. 12), and some of the original structure is probably incorporated in the two end walls. Potter's room is wider by about a third, extending the plan to the west to line up with the other rooms on the entrance front.

Some confusion surrounds the original function of the room. On Potter's designs it is called simply the 'Hall', but a bill submitted by him in 1798 describes it as 'the Drawing Room'. Yet other accounts call it the dining-room, and this it certainly was by 1842, when an inventory describes it as the 'Dining Hall', containing 36 single chairs and a 'sett of Dining Tables consisting of 8 tables with 2 leafs to each'. Furnished in this way, it must have looked more like a restaurant than an eating room in a private house.

In August 1821 a ball was held at Plas Newydd to celebrate the birthday of the newly crowned George IV, who was visiting Anglesey on his way to Ireland. The *North Wales Gazette* reported that '. . . the Grand Dining Hall was opened soon after 12 o'clock when the *Coup d'œil* was enchanting: tables were laid the entire length of that noble apartment and . . . what attracted the chief notice of the delighted guests was the confectionery which was displayed in an endless variety of ornaments, distributed with infinite taste throughout the several tables. . .' It must have been in this room that the thirteen-year-old Princess Victoria 'danced the gallop' in October 1832, and 'stayed up till near nine'.*

Decoration

It is not clear from the accounts whether the plasterwork 'vaulting' of the ceiling, with elaborate bosses at the intersection of the ribs, was carried out by 'Bernasconi's men', who certainly did the plasterwork of the Chapel in 1806–7, or by one 'Parratt the Plaisterer', to whom the large sum of £520 was still owing in 1812. Francis Bernasconi, from a family of Italian stuccadors originating near Lugano, worked with Wyatt at Belton in Lincolnshire (also NT) and elsewhere.

* Reproduced from Queen Victoria's *Journal,* 12 October 1832, by gracious permission of Her Majesty the Queen.

Chimney-piece

The finely carved chimney-piece with two fanciful medieval knights modelled in plaster for the niches to either side suggests a direct medieval source. A similar arrangement is found in the Drawing Room at Bodelwyddan Castle, Clwyd.

Paintings

Most of the paintings in the Music Room were seen here by J. P. Neale in 1822.

NORTH (FAR) WALL, ABOVE:

Studio of ALLAN RAMSAY (1713–84)

George III (1738–1820)

Ramsay was appointed Painter-in-Ordinary to the King in 1767 and '. . . conducted a sort of picture factory', from which he turned out Georges and Charlottes by the score, often for diplomatic use.

ISAAC POCOCK (1782–1835)

Henry Bayly, 9th Baron Paget, 1st Earl of Uxbridge (1744–1812)

See p. 63. Painted in his Peer's robes, with the old Houses of Parliament in the background. Exhibited posthumously at the RA, and possibly painted, in 1814.

Studio of ALLAN RAMSAY (1713–84)

Queen Charlotte (1744–1818)

Pendant to George III above.

DENIS DIGHTON (1792–1827)

The Final Charge of the British Cavalry at the Battle of Orthez

Signed and dated 1815

On 27 February 1814 the British and Spanish under Wellington defeated the French under Soult at Orthez in southern France. The future Marquess of Anglesey did not serve in this part of the Peninsular War. The commanders shown are Lord Edward Somerset and Lord Combermere (ironically, the man Wellington would have preferred above Anglesey to command the allied cavalry at Waterloo).

FIREPLACE WALL, ABOVE:

JOHN HOPPNER, RA (1758–1810)

Lady Caroline Capel (1773–1847) *and her daughter Harriet*

Exh. RA, 1794. The eldest sister of the 1st Marquess, she married the Hon. John Capel in 1792 and bore him thirteen children, of whom Harriet was the eldest. From 1814 to 1817 the family lived abroad for economic reasons, spending the Hundred Days (of the Waterloo campaign) in and around Brussels. Their letters home (published in 1955) give a fascinating flavour of those momentous events.

Sir THOMAS LAWRENCE, PRA (1769–1830)

Henry William, 1st Marquess of Anglesey, KG (1768–1854)

One of the greatest cavalry commanders of the Napoleonic era. Painted in his uniform as Colonel of the 7th Hussars (previously Light Dragoons) and wearing the Peninsular and Waterloo medals, and numerous Orders. Exh. RA, 1817. A replica commissioned by Wellington is at Apsley House.

JOHN HOPPNER, RA (1758–1810)

Lady Caroline Villiers, Lady Paget (1774–1835), *with her eldest son Henry* (1797–1869), 1800

'Car', the first wife of the future 1st Marquess of Anglesey. They were divorced in 1810 so that he could marry Lady Charlotte Wellesley ('Char'), and she the 6th Duke of Argyll (see p. 66).

(Opposite page) Conversation piece – the family of the 6th Marquess of Anglesey; begun by Rex Whistler in 1938 and never completed. Lady Caroline Paget leans against the doorway of the Music Room; the present Marquess paints at the easel; Lady Rose reads; the Marchioness plays the piano, watched by her daughters, Lady Mary and Lady Katharine; the 6th Marquess is seated in the armchair.

BELOW:

Attributed to CHARLES JERVAS
(1675?–1739)

Brigadier-General the Hon. Thomas Paget
(d. 1741)

Governor of Minorca. Grandson of the 5th Baron
Paget and father of Caroline Paget, Lady Bayly.

ENOCH SEEMAN (1690?–1745)

Unknown Lady

SOUTH (END) WALL, ABOVE:

JOHN HOPPNER, RA (1758–1810) and
SAWREY GILPIN, RA (1733–1807)

*Henry William, Lord Paget, later 1st Marquess of
Anglesey (1768–1854) as Lieut.-Colonel of the 7th
Light Dragoons (Hussars)*

Exh. RA, 1798.

Gilpin painted the horse, Hoppner the figure.

Attributed to Sir MARTIN ARCHER SHEE,
PRA (1769–1850)

General the Hon. Sir Edward Paget, GCB
(1775–1849)

A younger brother of the 1st Marquess. Lost his
arm before Oporto (1809), but later second-in-
command to Wellington in the Peninsula, until
captured by the French (1812–14). Later Commander-in-Chief in India (1822–5). Probably
painted shortly after his release in April 1814.

JOHN HOPPNER, RA (1758–1810)

The Hon. Sir Arthur Paget, GCB, PC
(1771–1840)

Diplomat and younger brother of the 1st Marquess. Painted c.1804 in the robes of the Order
of the Bath, to which he was appointed that year.
His gloomy dispatch after Napoleon's victory at
Austerlitz (1805) is said to have contributed to the
death of Pitt.

BELOW:

Manner of Sir ANTHONY VAN DYCK
(1599–1641)

*Lady Frances Devereux, Marchioness of Hertford
(later Duchess of Somerset) (1599–1674)*

Daughter of Elizabeth's unfortunate favourite, the
2nd Earl of Essex, and husband of the Royalist
commander.

GEORGE ROMNEY (1734–1802)

*Henry Bayly, 9th Baron Paget, 1st Earl of
Uxbridge (1744–1812)*

An unambitious man, friendly with George III
and fond of music. At 25 he inherited the Paget
barony through his mother, Caroline Paget. The
Uxbridge earldom was revived for him in 1784.
Father of the 1st Marquess of Anglesey.

   He holds in his left hand a sample of copper ore
from the mines at Parys Mountain near Amlwch,
where in 1785 he formed the Mona Mine Company. The revenues from it helped to finance his
remodelling of Plas Newydd in the 1790s.

Furniture

The two unusually large Sheraton-style mahogany-veneered side-tables have satinwood
inlays. There is also a set of twelve limed-oak armchairs upholstered in silk velvet,
French style, c.1725–50.

The 'boudoir' grand piano by John Broadwood (No.50378), c.1899, is shown with
some sheet music dedicated to the 5th Marquess (see p. 50).

The reduced, corona-shaped, partly gilt bronze chandelier is French Empire, c.1810.
The four Charles II-style plated sconces on the west (window) wall with cast decoration
surmounted by a marquess's coronet are part of a set of ten originally supplied for
the Long Gallery at Beaudesert (the others can be seen in the Octagon Room).

Clock

An ingenious and unusual Directoire plate glass 'skeleton' eight-day mantel clock with large Y-spoked great wheel and enamel chapter ring.

The Staircase Hall

Apart from the Gothick Hall, the Music Room and the Chapel (which no longer exists – see p. 46), all the other rooms decorated between 1793 and 1799 are in the Neo-classical taste more usually favoured by James Wyatt – a contrast in styles that the eighteenth century found perfectly acceptable. The surviving designs for the Staircase are probably by a draughtsman in the Wyatt office – they are not by either Wyatt or Potter. The work was supervised by Potter, whose June 1798 account details the construction of the two wooden fluted Doric columns, painted to resemble *verde antico* marble, and enriched with composition ornaments, in his workshop at Lichfield.

Taking advantage of an immensely thick outside wall, which both supported the cantilevered stairs and gave space for a vestibule from the secondary entrance below (see p. 11), the window is set in a curved recess over the middle flight, framed by two more Doric columns reflecting those on the landing opposite. The walls, like those of the Music Room and Gothick Hall, are of plaster, 'lined-out' to resemble stonework. The elegant wrought-iron and partly gilt bronze balustrade was supplied through Potter, but the maker is not known.

Paintings

SOUTH (MUSIC ROOM) WALL, BELOW:

Attributed to LEANDRO DA PONTE, called LEANDRO BASSANO (1558–1623)

A young Nobleman, said to be the 5th Baron Paget (1609–78), *c.*1620

Signed

The distant view of Venice and supposed identity of the sitter have led this picture being described as the earliest surviving 'Grand Tour' portrait. The dress suggests a non-Italian, but there is no evidence Lord Paget ever went to Italy.

ENGLISH, ? eighteenth-century

Nazareth Newton, Lady Paget

Married Thomas, 3rd Baron Paget in 1565. Though dated 1578, this is more probably a later pastiche of a sixteenth-century portrait. Purchased by the 6th Marquess in 1935 as a portrait of the 2nd Baron's wife, Katherine Knyvett (d. 1622). Formerly at the Knyvett house, Charlton Park, Wiltshire.

ABOVE:

Attributed to ENOCH SEEMAN (1690?–1745)

Caroline Paget, Lady Bayly (d. 1766)

For biography, see Gothick Hall above. Almost certainly a pendant to the probable portrait of Sir Nicholas Bayly.

Studio of Sir THOMAS LAWRENCE, PRA (1769–1830)

George IV (1762–1830)

A studio version of the 1814 portrait in the Marquess of Londonderry's collection. Painted in Field Marshal's uniform.

Attributed to ENOCH SEEMAN (1690?–1745)

Unknown Gentleman, probably Sir Nicholas Bayly, 2nd Bt (1709–82)

Much more probably the husband of, and pendant to, Caroline Paget, Lady Bayly, painted at the time of their marriage in 1737, than Thomas

The Staircase Hall

The Duke of Marlborough at the battle of Blenheim; by or after Louis Laguerre (Staircase Hall)

Catesby, Lord Paget (1689–1742), as traditionally claimed.

By or after LOUIS LAGUERRE (1663–1721)

Eight Battle Scenes after the Marlborough House Murals

These paintings are closely related to the mural decoration of the hall and staircase at Marlborough House in St James's, which Laguerre carried out for the great Duke of Marlborough in 1713, and they have previously been called sketches for this scheme. They seem more probably copies or reductions. The grained and gilt 'Greek key' frames, *c.*1770, have been adapted for their present location so as to cant the pictures downward.

RIGHT OF DOOR, ABOVE:

Three episodes from the battle of Blenheim, 1704

The attack on the village of Blenheim; a brigade of French Foot cut down when abandoned by their Horse; Prince Eugene of Savoy attacking the left wing of the French army.

BELOW:

Louis XIV with the French army at the battle of Ramillies, 1706

LEFT OF DOOR, ABOVE:

The Duke of Marlborough at the battle of Blenheim; the taking of Marshal Tallard and the pushing of 4,000 men into the Danube

BELOW:

The Duke of Marlborough at Blenheim

NORTH WALL, RIGHT TO LEFT:

The battle of Taniers (Malplaquet), 1709; the Duke of Marlborough and Prince Eugene entering the French entrenchments

The battle of Taniers (Malplaquet)

The pursuit of the French after the battle of Ramillies

WEST WALL:

The Duke of Marlborough at Blenheim

25

JOHN VANDERBANK (1694–1739)

Philip Dormer Stanhope, 4th Earl of Chesterfield (1694–1773), *c.*1730

Statesman, diplomat and writer to his son of letters of worldly advice, which Dr Johnson thought 'teach the morals of a whore and the manners of a dancing-master'.

JOHN LUCAS, RA (1807–74)

Arthur Wellesley, 1st Duke of Wellington (1769–1852)

Commissioned in 1840 by the 1st Marquess and completed two years later. The Duke was 'much flattered by [Lord Anglesey's] desire to possess a portrait of me, and you may rely upon every exertion on my part, that you should have the best that can be painted at present'. He wrote to the artist in December 1841: 'I beg you to recollect . . . how desirable it is to attend to the size of the head . . . the Head of those you have painted even that in the robes of the Chancellor of Oxford is too large; I always thought so; and you may rely upon it I am right'. This letter, which suggests that the Duke would have been happier to sit once more for Sir Thomas Lawrence (had he not died ten years earlier), is displayed on one of the tables below, with a full transcript.

JOHN VANDERBANK (1694–1739)

Francis North, 1st Earl of Guilford (1704–90)

Signed and dated 1736

Father of George III's Prime Minister, Lord North.

EAST WALL (LANDING):

ENGLISH, eighteenth-century, after HOLBEIN (1497/8–1543)

Henry VIII (1491–1547)

ENGLISH, sixteenth-century

William, 1st Baron Paget (1505/6–63)

Wearing the jewel of the Order of the Garter. Bears a later inscription and date, 1549.

ENGLISH, sixteenth-century

Queen Elizabeth (1533–1603)

Derived from Isaac Oliver's unsparing miniature of the aging Queen, of *c.*1592. Note the 'moon-jewel' in her hair, alluding to the cult of her as the virgin goddess of the moon, Diana or Cynthia.

ENGLISH, 1585?

Unknown Gentleman, aged 30

The chief arms appear to be those of the Winnington family, of Winnington Hall, Cheshire.

Document

The framed vellum document under the stairs is a Patent of Edward VI dated 1553, granting arms to William, 1st Baron Paget.

Furniture, ceramics and glass

A set of four upright armchairs, French, *c.*1670, with walnut frames and modern upholstery.

A pair of unusual George III Neo-classical giltwood console-tables with ram's head ornaments, *c.*1800. The tables probably had marble tops originally, and the ornament of the frieze, in the form of *paterae* or continuous guilloche, is missing. The tables were formerly at Beaudesert, but may originally have been supplied for Uxbridge House, the family's London home, which was begun in 1792.

The chandelier is English, *c.*1835.

The nineteenth-century Chinese blue-and-white baluster vase, Kangxi, c.1700, has a japanned wooden knop, replaced in the early nineteenth century. It stands on a carved walnut base c.1690, probably Italian, from the Veneto.

ON LANDING:

A Neo-classical-style painted and giltwood pier-glass.

A George III giltwood side-table with mottled green marble top.

A pair of George III restored beechwood children's chairs.

A Chinese pagoda of carved ivory, c.1830, stands between two Chinese soapstone pagodas.

Clock

A George I eight-day longcase clock by Robert Henderson of Scarborough, the case japanned in green and gold, c.1730. The maker was a Quaker and died in 1756.

Carpet

The Wilton hand-knotted carpet and stair-carpet were laid in 1914.

The Middle Landing

Painting

ENGLISH, nineteenth-century

Henry, Earl of Uxbridge, later 2nd Marquess of Anglesey (1797–1869)

A *roué* who lived in the shadow of his famous father, the 1st Marquess.

Chalk drawings

FRANCIS WILLIAM WILKIN (c.1790–1842)

Seven chalk portraits of the children of Henry William, 1st Marquess of Anglesey and Lady Caroline Villiers, his first wife, 1823:

FROM RIGHT TO LEFT, ALONG CORRIDOR:

Lord Arthur Paget (1805–25)

A favourite of his father, Lord Arthur died after a hunting accident only a month before his twentieth birthday.

Lady Caroline Paget, Duchess of Richmond (1796–1874)

Henry, Earl of Uxbridge, later 2nd Marquess of Anglesey (1797–1869)

Signed and dated 1823

Lady Georgiana Paget, later Lady Crofton (1800–75)

Lady Jane Paget, later Lady Conyngham (1798–1876)

Lady Augusta Paget, later Lady Templemore (1802–72)

Lord William Paget (1803–73)

The black sheep of the family, a spendthrift who was the cause of continual anguish to his father.

Watercolours

JOHN 'WARWICK' SMITH (1749–1831)

*Seven views of Plas Newydd and surroundings, and a view of Beaudesert, c.*1800

LEFT TO RIGHT ALONG CORRIDOR:

Plas Newydd from the North

Wyatt and Potter's chapel can be seen on the right.

Plas Newydd from the South

A rare glimpse of the garden planting can be seen on the left, and on the right the coastal landscape before the advent of bridges and pylons.

Plas Newydd from the North

Almost the opposite view to the previous picture, probably made on Craig-y-Dinas, the rocky eminence on which the Anglesey Column was later to be erected.

Beaumaris Castle and town from the park at Baron Hill

The ruined thirteenth-century castle served as an 'eyecatcher' from the house built for the Bulkeley family by Samuel Wyatt in the 1770s. The buildings to the left may represent – with some inaccuracy as to precise location – Penmon Priory.

Beaudesert, Staffordshire

The principal seat of the Pagets from the mid-sixteenth century until it was demolished in 1935.

At the time of this view Cannock Chase, much of which was Paget land, preserved the character of an ancient forest.

View towards Snowdon

From the Plas Newydd estate south of the house.

View towards the Carneddau

From the Plas Newydd estate, a small quarry in the foreground.

View towards the Rivals

From the Plas Newydd estate.

STAIRS TO HALF-LANDING:

ENGLISH, *c.*1810

Two views of Beaudesert, Staffordshire

ENGLISH, *c.*1817

Plas Newydd from the South-west

Humphry Repton's screen-plantings appear well-advanced.

Lord Anglesey's Column

Designed by Thomas Harrison of Chester and set up in 1817 to honour the hero of Waterloo.

Clock

The eight-day striking spring clock in an ebonised case is by Edward and Hatley Moore of Ipswich, *c.*1770.

The Gothick Hall Gallery

Paintings

ENGLISH, eighteenth-century

Mary Tudor (1516–58)

An imaginary, sixteenth-century-style portrait.

After Sir PETER LELY (1618–80)

Edward Montagu, 1st Earl of Sandwich (1625–72)

The admiral who conveyed Charles II to England in 1660. Killed at the battle of Solebay.

Sir James Jebusa Shannon, RA (1862–1923)

Lady Winifred Paget, Viscountess Ingestre, and her infant son, later 21st Earl of Shrewsbury

Lady Winifred was the daughter of Lord Alexander Paget, and the aunt of the present Marquess of Anglesey.

The Hon. Henry Graves (1818–82)

Lady Florence Paget as a girl (1842–81), 1850

The youngest daughter of the 2nd Marquess, she became a famous beauty, of whom *The Queen* wrote in 1863, 'Her petite figure and dove-like eyes caused her at once to become the rage of the park, the ball-room and the croquet lawn.'

Known as 'the Pocket Venus', she was the notorious object of rivalry between Henry Chaplin and the 4th Marquess of Hastings. In 1864, when engaged to the first, she went out to buy her wedding trousseau, gave her chaperone the slip, and was driven to St George's, Hanover Square to marry Hastings. He died four years later, ruined by gambling debts and the last of his line. After two years she remarried another gambler, Sir George Chetwynd, 4th Bt.

Graves was the 1st Marquess's nephew. Several of his affectionate sketches of the elderly Marquess can be seen in the Cavalry Museum.

Rex Whistler (1905–44)

Charles, 6th Marquess of Anglesey (1885–1947), c.1937

An unfinished version of the portrait of Lord Anglesey as Chancellor of the University College of North Wales, Bangor.

Rex Whistler (1905–44)

Lady Caroline Paget (1913–76), c.1938

Eldest daughter of the 6th Marquess. Married Sir Michael Duff, Bt, of Vaynol (opposite Plas Newydd), in 1949. One of several portraits of Lady Caroline, with whom the artist was in love (see Saloon and Rex Whistler Exhibition).

Furniture

A small composite walnut-veneered bureau probably made up in the 1930s from a George I kneehole desk and the top from a slightly earlier bureau cabinet.

Lady Anglesey's Bedroom

This room occupies the first floor of the octagonal south-east tower, built by Sir Nicholas Bayly in 1753. The bay window at the far end gives magnificent views along the Menai Strait towards Caernarfon with the little harbour built by Lord Uxbridge in 1796 in the foreground; the other window looks northwards towards Stephenson's Britannia Bridge.

Decoration

The plasterwork frieze of loose acanthus scrolls and caryatids, and the chaste Neo-classical chimney-piece, are part of the redecoration of the house by Wyatt and Potter between 1793 and 1799, but the present colour scheme of pale pinks and whites was introduced by Lady Marjorie Manners, wife of the 6th Marquess, with the advice of Sibyl Colefax, one of the leading decorators of the inter-war period. The muslin bedhangings and curtains, the floral chintzes and the wallpaper with a pattern like gathered drapery, all somewhat faded after nearly sixty years, admirably reflect the taste of the 1930s.

Paintings and drawings

CONSTANT JOSEPH BROCHART (1816–99)

Confidences

Pastel

CONSTANT JOSEPH BROCHART (1816–99)

A Pet Bird

Pastel

ENGLISH, nineteenth-century

A Young Girl

Pastel

JACQUES EMILE BLANCHE (1861–1942)

Lady Marjorie Manners, later Marchioness of Anglesey (1883–1946)

Painted in 1909, three years before her marriage to Charles, 6th Marquess of Anglesey.

Sculpture

To the right of the door is an eighteenth-century Italian gilt-bronze relief of the Virgin and Child, in a later, nineteenth-century, cast metal surround. The serpent (with a man's head) crushed beneath the Virgin's feet is usually found in representations of the Virgin of the Immaculate Conception.

Furniture

The beechwood bed, naturalistically painted with trailing ivy, acanthus and husks on the posts and cornices, is in the Sheraton-style, *c*.1800. The present hangings were made up by Sybil Colefax.

On the wall to either side of the bed are two rococo giltwood girandoles, almost exactly drawn from plate 178 in Thomas Chippendale's *Gentleman & Cabinet Maker's Director* of 1762. The overmantel looking-glass mirror bears a similarly close resemblance to plate 179. They may date from the twentieth-century redecoration of the room.

The polychrome and gilt figures of Nubian slaves bearing baskets of fruit on their heads are probably Venetian.

The white-painted open armchair with reeded rails and turned and carved uprights is in the Sheraton-style of the late eighteenth century.

The painted armchair with a circular pierced back in the George III style may have been decorated by Rex Whistler.

Clock

The eight-day bronze and ormolu French mantel clock in the form of a Turk riding a mule is unsigned, French, *c*.1815.

Lady Anglesey's Bedroom

Ceramics and glass

An early nineteenth-century Paris *jardinière* with painted reserves of Napoleonic soldiers.

A pair of Victorian cut-glass two-tier lustres.

A George III-style English glass chandelier.

Lord Anglesey's Bedroom

The plaster frieze, with its honeysuckle pattern, belongs to the 1790s, as does the chimney-piece of Volterra and Siena marbles (perhaps the stones recorded in the accounts as being supplied by Benjamin Bromfield of Liverpool, who also furnished chimney-pieces for Chirk Castle). This bedroom was used by the present Marquess until 1976, when he gave Plas Newydd to the National Trust. The stately bathroom exemplifies Lord Anglesey's father's dictum that 'every bathroom should have a bedroom'.

Paintings

The collection of marine paintings reflects the long-established naval and maritime interests of the family.

CLOCKWISE, BEGINNING OVER BATHROOM DOOR:

ENGLISH, nineteenth-century

A fishing boat beached on a rocky coast

WILLIAM ADOLPHUS KNELL (*c.*1805–75)

Shipping off the Cornish Coast, 1869
Signed

St Michael's Mount appears at the left of the picture.

BELOW:

DUTCH, nineteenth-century

Shipping in a calm sea

ABOVE:

ENGLISH, nineteenth-century

An engagement between French and British men-of-war

BELOW:

JAMES ROGERS (1838–96)

The yacht 'Pearl'

OVERMANTEL:

BENJAMIN MARSHALL (1768–1835)

The Duke of Richmond's 'Rough Robin' with a jockey up, 1830
Signed

The presence of this picture at Plas Newydd may be due to the marriage in 1817 of Lady Caroline Paget, eldest daughter of the 1st Marquess, to the 5th Duke of Richmond.

ABOVE:

ENGLISH, nineteenth-century

'La Sybil', a man-of-war at anchor off Gibraltar

A command of Lord William Paget, the 1st Marquess's second son.

JAMES ROGERS (1838–96)

The yacht 'Pearl'

Companion to the picture on the other side of the fireplace.

ENGLISH, nineteenth-century

Men-of-war becalmed at anchor, with fishermen and boats on the beach

ON LANDING OUTSIDE:

One of the coloured aquatint portraits represents Mrs Rosoman Mountain (1768–1848), among the foremost singers of her day, after a portrait by J.J. Masquerier; her male companion is not Mr Mountain (a violinist).

State bed

The state bed of *c.*1720 came from the other Paget house, Beaudesert in Staffordshire, after its demolition in 1935. It is of the type known as an 'angel' or flying-tester bedstead, since the tester is hung from the ceiling and not supported by footposts. It is covered in exceptionally beautiful Chinese silk painted with flowers, which originally echoed the Chinese export wallpaper of the State Bedroom at Beaudesert.

During a fire there in 1909 the bed was badly damaged by water, and extensive restoration was required. When it was moved to Plas Newydd, the headboard, with its central recess lined with silver braid, had to be somewhat reduced in height. By then the curtains were thought to be beyond repair, and so the sections in good condition were used to

Lord Anglesey's Bedroom

make a large pelmet board extending over both the windows in this room, and echoing the shape of the cornice of the bed.

Other furniture

The other furniture is mostly mid-Georgian and includes a pair of mahogany kneehole dressing-tables, some splat-back chairs and a mahogany boot-jack. There is also a twentieth-century George III-style break-front wardrobe.

The brass chandelier is Dutch, eighteenth-century. On one of the dressing-tables is a luxurious travelling dressing-case by Jenner & Newstub of Jermyn St, which probably belonged to the flamboyant 5th Marquess. If so, it is one of his few possessions that escaped the 40-day sale following his death in 1905.

Clock

The eight-day French mantel clock, with a bronze group of one of the 'Marly horses' after Coustou, is signed 'Delaunay à Paris', *c*.1825.

Visitors should now descend the spiral staircase to re-enter the Gothick Hall. Those who would prefer not to use this stair are asked to contact one of the room stewards.

The Gothick Hall

Paintings

LEFT OF DOOR, ABOVE:

ENGLISH, *c*.1650

Lady Elizabeth Cavendish, Countess of Bridgewater (1625/6–63)

Daughter of the 1st Duke of Newcastle and wife (m.1641) of the 2nd Earl of Bridgewater. Her great-granddaughter, Lady Elizabeth Egerton, married Thomas, Lord Paget in 1718.

BELOW:

FRENCH, *c*.1670

Princess Henrietta Stuart, Duchess of Orleans (1644–70)

'Minette', the favourite sister of Charles II and wife of Philip, Duke of Orleans, the brother of Louis XIV.

RIGHT OF DOOR, ABOVE:

EDWARD H. MAY (1824–87)

Henrietta Bagot, Countess of Uxbridge (1815–44), *c*.1840

Daughter of Sir Charles Bagot of Blithfield, Staffordshire. Married Henry, Earl of Uxbridge (later 2nd Marquess of Anglesey) in 1833 (as his second wife).

BELOW:

ENGLISH, *c*.1650

Unknown Lady

Traditionally called Anne Carr (Countess of Bedford), but bearing no resemblance to her.

OVER DOOR:

After ? CORNELIUS JONSON (1593–1661)

Unknown Gentleman, c.1627–8

The Ante-Room

The large door which gives out on to the lawn leading down to the Strait typifies the coalition of styles at Plas Newydd, being emphatically Gothick on the outside, yet on its inner face perfectly in accord with the correct Neo-classicism of the rest of the room, which was designed by James Wyatt in 1795. The decoration dates from the 1930s.

Paintings

SOUTH (RIGHT) WALL:

Sir THOMAS LAWRENCE, PRA (1769–1830)
The Hon. Berkeley Paget, MP (1780–1842)
Sixth son of the 1st Earl of Uxbridge. Probably painted *c.*1807.

NORTH (LEFT) WALL:

ENGLISH, *c.*1760s
Henry Bayly, 9th Baron Paget, later 1st Earl of Uxbridge (1744–1812)
Previously thought to have been painted by Pompeo Batoni in the course of the sitter's Grand Tour, but in fact done in Britain – just possibly by Giuseppe Marchi (1721/22–1808), on his brief attempt to break free from Reynolds's studio and create his own practice in Wales, in 1768–9.

Furniture

The set of Louis XV painted armchairs is upholstered in a *toile de Jouy* (copperplate-printed linen) based on an early eighteenth-century design, 'Old Ford' by Robert Jones, which is also used for the curtains.

The pair of gilt console-tables with arched supports is in the style of John Gumley and James Moore, two of the leading English cabinetmakers of the first quarter of the eighteenth century, who supplied similar pieces for Hampton Court and for Boughton House in Northamptonshire. Their tops, painted to resemble black marble, are later, *c.*1750. The tall pier-glasses in narrow gesso frames above them are late nineteenth- or early twentieth-century; the Paget crest has been painted on the medallions in their crestings. Both tables and glasses came from Beaudesert.

The plaster-framed pier-glasses on the outer wall are twentieth-century. Below them is a pair of late George III pier-tables, made from dining-table ends and later painted.

Ceramics

On the painted pier-tables is a pair of green-ground vases with Napoleonic scenes.

The blue-and-white *jardinières* on the opposite tables are Chinese, late nineteenth- to early twentieth-century.

The Octagon Room

Occupying the ground floor of the south-east tower, the room was given this name in nineteenth-century inventories. It was used until recently as Lady Anglesey's study. The frieze here is identical to that in the Ante-Room, designed by Wyatt in 1795, though here it is picked out against a striking red background, again dating from the 1930s.

It was against the south-east corner of this room that Humphry Repton, in his 'Red Book' of 1799, proposed to build an octagonal Gothick conservatory, its windows removable in the summer ('The principal apartments are all ensuite & by large folding doors a very fine enfilade is preserved thro' the whole building, which I suppose was to be increased in the usual way by a large looking glass; but instead of this, I think a small conservatory or greenhouse might be added to the end drawing room. . .'). The idea was never adopted, but it was published as an engraving in Repton's *Theory and Practice of Landscape Gardening* in 1803.

Chimney-piece

The white marble chimney-piece is almost certainly the 'Reeded Chimney' bought by Lord Uxbridge for £45 'at Mr Westmacotts, Mount St, Grosvenor Sq', on 2 March 1796. Richard Westmacott the Elder (1747–1808), father of the more famous sculptor of that name, is recorded several times as supplying chimney-pieces for houses with which James Wyatt was concerned, and his appearance in the Plas Newydd accounts supports the idea that Wyatt was the principal architect, with Potter as executant, or assistant, architect.

Doors

This room, like several others in the house, has a double doorway fitted with 'sympathetic hinges': when one door is opened or closed, the other moves in concert with it (thanks to a mechanism under the floor). The invention, of which few examples survive in country houses, is credited to Samuel Wyatt, James's brother and also a successful architect.

Paintings

FIREPLACE WALL:

CHARLES MARTIN POWELL (1775–1824)

Fishermen and boats with two sailing ships beyond

Powell was a sailor and self-taught painter who fell into the clutches of dealers, and consequently died in penury.

GEORGE ARNALD, ARA (1763–1841)

The Menai Bridge, 1828

The bridge is seen from the mainland looking south-west; Plas Newydd is indicated in the very centre of the picture. The masterpiece of the Scottish engineer Thomas Telford, it was completed in 1826, and was by far the widest suspension bridge at the time. Prior to its construction the quickest ferry crossing took forty minutes.

The 1st Marquess at first opposed the project, but later agreed on condition that some rocks in the narrow passage of the Strait were blown up so as to ensure safe navigation.

In the 1930s the chains were replaced and the deck radically altered. The contemporary suspension bridge at Conwy, also by Telford, is now the property of the National Trust.

The Octagon Room

? 'J.W', ENGLISH, nineteenth-century

*A fishing boat with a warship at anchor off Dover,
1800?*

The artist with this monogram is unknown.

RIGHT OF DOOR:

GEORGE NAIRN (1799–1850)

Lord Anglesey's horse 'Cossack', 1828

Signed

Painted in Dublin when the 1st Marquess was
Lord Lieutenant of Ireland.

LEFT WALL:

Sir JAMES JEBUSA SHANNON, RA
(1862–1923)

Violet, Duchess of Rutland (1856–1937)

Lady Violet was a talented amateur artist and a
member of the 'Souls', a group of intellectually
minded aristocrats active at the turn of the century. Grandmother to the present Marquess. The
Duchess was painted more than once by Shannon,
and in this picture, painted for her daughter
Marjorie (see below) she appears 'as Russian or
Charity', in 'a Mucha-like headdress'.

Sir JAMES JEBUSA SHANNON, RA
(1862–1923)

*Lady Marjorie Manners, later Marchioness of
Anglesey* (1883–1946), *aged seventeen*, 1900

A replica of a portrait at Belvoir Castle, the
Manners' seat in Rutland. Mother of the present
Marquess.

BETWEEN WINDOWS, LEFT:

ENGLISH, *c*.1800, after WILLIAM SCROTS
(fl.1537–53)

Edward VI (1537–53)

Perhaps, with the following picture, from a set of
'historical' portraits.

RIGHT:

ENGLISH, *c*.1800, after HOLBEIN
(1497/8–1543)
Henry VIII (1491–1547)
See previous picture.

Furniture

The furniture includes more of the set of painted Louis XV seat furniture seen in the Ante-Room, upholstered in another *toile de Jouy* of a different pattern. The same material is also used for the curtains and pelmets, this time with a nautical design appropriate to the constantly changing views of shipping seen from the windows.

Much of the furniture is of the Regency or George IV periods, including the mahogany-veneered upright bookcase with burr yew inlays and ebony stringing, a writing-table with a brass lattice gallery, a japanned adjustable music stand, and an Irish pedestal table inscribed: 'part of an oak tree dug up from an Irish Bog, 90 feet tall & 5 feet diameter'. It was a gift to the 1st Marquess from Valentine, Lord Cloncurry, his close friend and political adviser when Lord Lieutenant of Ireland in 1828 and 1830–4.

The early twentieth-century terrestrial globe on a nineteenth-century mahogany tripod stand is by W. & A. K. Johnston of Edinburgh and London, and the carved and giltwood pier-glass to the left of the door is early George II, *c*.1730, in the style of William Kent.

The white-painted and gilt games tables in the Régence taste flanking the fireplace are French, *c*.1890. One has a conventional ebony and satinwood chessboard top; the other chessboard is set within needlework panels of the lions and eagles of the Pagets' arms, worked in *demi point* in the 1930s.

The plated sconces are part of the set also seen in the Music Room, and the six-light chandelier is one of a set of four also originally supplied for Beaudesert.

Bronzes

On the games tables are a statuette of the 1st Marquess as General of Hussars by William Theed (1804–91), and a cast of Canova's bust of Napoleon.

Ceramics

The Samson porcelain on the mantelpiece dates from the end of the nineteenth century, imitating the style of *c*.1770.

Photographs

The photograph on the table shows the house from the Strait in about 1890. On the wall to either side of the fireplace are group portraits of four of the present Marquess's sisters, Lady Caroline, Lady Elizabeth, Lady Mary and Lady Rose, taken in about 1930. To the right of the fireplace a photograph, taken by Marcus Adams in 1924, shows the present Marquess aged two and his twin sister Lady Katharine (Kitty).

The Saloon

The semicircular bay window, giving panoramic views over the Menai Strait, occupies the ground floor of the round tower which Sir Nicholas Bayly added to the east front of the old house in 1751, the first phase of the Gothick remodelling of Plas Newydd. The plan of the room probably also dates from this time; Sir Nicholas Bayly's letters to John Cartwright at Plas Newydd in 1751 refer to 'the great room', and 'the rooms over the great room & turret room'.

Decoration

The plaster frieze, moulded in the form of garlands of flowers held by ribbons, the guilloche mouldings around the windows, and the panelled mahogany double doors are from Lord Uxbridge's later re-edification of the room, corresponding exactly with two designs for the 'Drawing Room' made by James Wyatt in 1795. The doors themselves were made at a cost of £57 in Joseph Potter's Lichfield workshops in 1798, when the room must have been more or less completed; the walls were hung with what was described as an 'India' (ie Chinese) painted silk taffeta, 'a present from the Queen', finished off with 'Brass rods round the Room to preserve the silk' (1803

The Saloon

Inventory), and the same material was used for the curtains. Lord and Lady Uxbridge were closely acquainted with George III and Queen Charlotte (see p.64).

In the 1840s Thomas Assheton Smith of Vaynol, who had leased Plas Newydd from the 1st Marquess, asked permission to remove the silk hangings from this and several other rooms. Whilst agreeing to this elsewhere, Lord Anglesey replied that he was anxious to keep 'Queen Charlotte's silk'. Even so, this exceedingly rich scheme lasted barely a hundred years, and a photograph of 1896 shows painted walls and a stencilled ceiling. It also shows one of Wyatt's original doorcases with garlanded architraves, which had to be removed in the 1930s, when the four large landscapes by Ommeganck (see below) were introduced.

Like many of the rooms, the present arrangement of the Saloon and the hanging of the pictures reflect to a large extent the taste of Lady Marjorie Manners and her husband, the 6th Marquess of Anglesey, who in the 1930s entirely redecorated the house, and placed the furniture newly arrived from Beaudesert. The comfort and informality of the rooms as they left them, with fitted Wilton carpets, and curtains and upholstery in warm complementary tones, were in many ways in advance of their time.

Chimney-piece

The white marble chimney-piece, with panels of guilloche ornament at the sides matching the window surrounds, is the most elaborate of its kind in the house, and is almost certainly the one bought by Lord Uxbridge from Richard Westmacott the Elder in 1796, for the large sum of £120.

Paintings

The four enormous paintings of pastoral scenes with peasants and animals which dominate the room are by the Flemish artist Balthasar Paul Ommeganck (1755–1826), two of them dated 1789, and must originally have formed the entire decoration of a room in the Netherlands. They were introduced in a more spaced-out arrangement here in the 1930s.

CLOCKWISE, FROM OVER DOOR TO ANTE-ROOM:

ANONYMOUS, eighteenth- or nineteenth-century

A Venetian Capriccio

A view looking towards the Lagoon, with part of the Old Library of St Mark's on the right.

ENGLISH, ? eighteenth-century

A Castle on a rocky coast

The castle shows some similarities with Conwy, but the setting does not correspond.

RICHARD BARRETT DAVIS (1782–1854)

Queen Victoria and her suite riding out in Windsor Great Park, 1839

An engraved key to the picture may be seen to the left of the fireplace. Immediately behind the Queen are her uncle, King Leopold of the Belgians and his Queen, and (on the grey horse) Lord Uxbridge, later 2nd Marquess of Anglesey, at that time Lord Chamberlain. His younger brother, Lord Alfred Paget, an equerry from 1837 to 1877, is also of the party. Exh. RA, 1841.

Davis was the son and brother of royal huntsmen at Windsor, and had been Animal Painter to William IV.

The Saloon in 1896

NETHERLANDISH, seventeenth-century

A village street with a performing bear

An imaginary scene by a Dutch or Flemish artist working in, or from memories of, Italy.

NETHERLANDISH, seventeenth-century

Figures, animals and waggons crossing a ford

Pendant to the above.

RICHARD DIGHTON (1795–1880)

A coloured lithograph of the 3rd Marquess on a grey horse, from the series *Equestrian Sketches*, and a watercolour of the same sitter driving. Dighton made several likenesses of the Marquess, some of which can be seen in the Cavalry Museum.

WILLIAM HENRY DAVIS (*c.*1795–1885)

The 1st Marquess of Anglesey shooting blackcock on Cannock Chase, 1830

Signed

Lord Anglesey remained an active horseman long after losing his leg at Waterloo (see p. 66). Beside him is his dog, 'Nep'.

W. H. Davis was also Animal Painter to William IV, but seems not to have been related to R. B. Davis, as sometimes said.

ANONYMOUS, eighteenth- or nineteenth-century

A Venetian Capriccio

A canal scene, with part of the Doge's Palace at left.

ON TABLE:

REX WHISTLER (1905–44)

Lady Caroline Paget (1913–76)

Pencil drawing

One of several portraits of Lady Caroline by her close friend.

41

FLEMISH, sixteenth-century

Portrait of an Unknown Man, called William, 1st Baron Paget de Beaudesert (1505/6–63)

ENGLISH, ? sixteenth-century

Stephen Gardiner, Bishop of Winchester (?1483–1555)

Cardinal Wolsey's secretary and much involved in the divorce of Anne Boleyn. Imprisoned under Edward VI for opposing doctrinal reform; persecutor of Protestants under Mary. The 1st Baron Paget (see p.59) was a protégé and later rival. The prime version is at Trinity Hall, Cambridge, where Gardiner was Master and Paget an undergraduate.

Sculpture

On marble half-columns to either side of the central bay are two busts by Sir William Reid Dick, RA (1879–1961), the bronze of Marjorie, Marchioness of Anglesey, made in 1925, and the marble of her eldest daughter, Lady Caroline Paget, in 1923.

Furniture

At either end of the room is an unusual George II carved and giltwood pier-table, *c.*1730, somewhat in the manner of Kent, but with supports in the manner of sea-lions. They came from Ingestre Hall, the home of the Talbot family in Staffordshire, where they had been painted brown and used as supports for a dining-table.

Above them are two gilt gesso pier-glasses with the same provenance, similar in form, but with many differences in the details, French, *c.*1720.

The pair of giltwood pier-glasses with unusual 'budding' terminals to the broken pediments is George II, and has been altered substantially.

The later Georgian furniture includes a George III mahogany-veneered rent table (which originally would have stood in the agent's office) with alphabetically lettered drawers for the records of each tenant, and a cylindrical box in the centre of the top to take the rental moneys. To the right of the fireplace there is a 'Chinese Chippendale'-style side-table on a twentieth-century base.

To the right of the bay window is a Regency 'chiffonier' bookcase, veneered in rosewood, with black painted and gilt columns at the angles, of a type described by the designer George Smith in 1810 as being 'used chiefly for such books as are in constant use, and not of sufficient consequence for the library'. The olivewood-veneered circular table on a triple pedestal is probably Maltese, *c.*1820.

Beyond it is a mahogany artist's or architect's table of about 1760, with a facsimile of one of the plates from *The Britannia & Conway Tubular Bridges* by Edwin Clarke, Resident Engineer, 1850. The elegant profile of Robert Stephenson's Britannia Bridge can now be appreciated only from these engravings, since it was rebuilt after a fire in 1970.

Along the inside wall are several George I walnut chairs, their floral embroidered seats worked in the 1930s by the 6th Marquess and his friends.

Clock

The eight-day German mantel clock in an ebonised case on the mantelpiece is unsigned, *c*.1890.

Ceramics and glass

On one of the pier-tables is a Chinese *famille rose* footbath, late Qianlong, *c*.1770, and the garniture of vases and ice-cream buckets on the mantelpiece dates from *c*.1900.

The single engraved glass candle-shade on a glass base on the chiffonier is English, late George III.

Photographs

Distributed around the room are photographs of the family, their houses, and royalty including George V and Queen Mary, and the present Royal Family during a visit to Plas Newydd in 1958. Lord Anglesey appears in two photographs: one taken when he appeared with the Duke of Edinburgh in a television programme during the Year of the Environment; and, with Mr Peter Chance, taken at the time of his gift of Plas Newydd to the National Trust in 1976. A photograph taken at the end of the last century shows four gardeners posing during the work of scything the great lawn before the days of mowing machines, and the photograph of Beaudesert was taken at the time of the (abortive) 1924 sale.

The Breakfast Room

Originally known as the 'North Ante-Room', since it mirrors what is still called the Ante-Room at the other end of the Saloon, this room was also the work of James Wyatt. The frieze is of the same pattern as those of the Octagon and Ante-Rooms, and follows Wyatt's signed drawing of 1795. The five pairs of doors with their high architraves were included in Joseph Potter's bill for joinery in 1798, and the white marble chimney-piece is probably again by Westmacott.

Paintings

Three famous marine artists are represented by two pictures each.

NORTH AND SOUTH WALLS:

LEFT:

JOHN THOMAS SERRES (1759–1825)
Men-of-war and other shipping in a calm, with fishermen in front
Signed and dated 1816

RIGHT:

JOHN THOMAS SERRES (1759–1825)
Fishing boats in a breeze off Great Yarmouth
Signed and dated 1816

WEST WALL, FACING WINDOWS:

LEFT:

PETER MONAMY (1681–1749)
A man-of-war firing a salute in a calm

RIGHT:

PETER MONAMY (1681–1749)
George II in the Royal Yacht on a return from Hanover

EAST, WINDOW, WALL:

LEFT:

NICHOLAS POCOCK (1741–1821)
Ships in the Menai Strait
Watercolour
Signed and dated 1804

RIGHT:

NICHOLAS POCOCK (1741–1821)
A man-of-war and other shipping off the Welsh coast
Watercolour
Signed

Sculpture

IVOR ROBERTS-JONES (b. 1916)
Henry, 7th Marquess of Anglesey (b. 1922)
Bronze
Commissioned by the National Trust in 1978.

MATTHEW NOBLE (1818–76)
Fitzroy Richard Clarence Paget
Dated 1859

Furniture

The mahogany breakfast-table opposite the fireplace is close to a design (plate 33) in the third edition of Chippendale's *Director*, published in 1762. The wire mesh underneath was designed to protect food from the attentions of domestic pets.

The Rex Whistler Exhibition

Divided earlier this century into two rooms, a kitchen and a pantry, this was formerly the billiard room, built on to the house in 1783–5, when Lord Uxbridge commissioned the mason John Cooper to erect a second octagonal tower at this end of the east front to balance Sir Nicholas Bayly's (of 1753) at the other end – the present Octagon Room. The frieze and two niches are obviously of a piece with Wyatt's decoration of the other rooms along this front, and must date from between 1795 and 1798.

The room is now devoted to the work of Rex Whistler, the artist whose close friendship with the Paget family in the 1930s resulted in one of the chief glories of the house, the long Dining Room which lies beyond, its walls entirely painted by him in *trompe-l'œil*.

The exhibition embraces Whistler's work as a portraitist, book illustrator, stage designer, decorative artist and amateur architect, as well as *personalia* and correspondence, and as the collection increases it is intended to become the principal *corpus* of his work in the country. The plaster urns in the niches were copied by Christopher Hobbs in 1977 from a pair that Whistler designed for Samuel Courtauld's London house. Around each is a frieze of figures of historical Samuels.

Reginald John (Rex) Whistler was born at Eltham in Kent in 1905, the son of a builder and great-great-grandson of perhaps England's greatest silversmith, Paul Storr (but not directly related to the American painter J. A. McNeill Whistler). He showed a talent for drawing at a very early age (some of his school work can be seen in the exhibition) and never intended to be anything but an artist. On leaving Haileybury he was accepted by the Royal Academy Schools, but (being entirely self-taught) rejected after one term. However, Professor Henry Tonks, Principal at the Slade School, saw his promise in a moment and was delighted to accept him. It was Tonks who secured for Whistler his first major commission (at the age of only twenty), to decorate the new restaurant at the Tate Gallery. This established his reputation in the art of mural painting and led to many subsequent commissions, besides his masterpiece in this form, the Plas Newydd Dining Room.

Whistler's visionary, arcadian style found great favour in Britain in the inter-war years, and his work as an illustrator of books (in which his masterpiece, *Gulliver's Travels* of 1930, is represented at Plas Newydd by the proof plates as well as a copy of the book) and

Proof for plate 4 of
Rex Whistler's illustrated
Gulliver's Travels, 1930
(Rex Whistler Exhibition)

designer in the theatre, opera, ballet and film, was extraordinarily prolific. His career was tragically cut short by an enemy mortar as he sought to clear the ensnared track of one of his troop of tanks in Normandy in July 1944.

Some of the exhibits are on loan from the artist's great friend, the present Marquess.

The Rex Whistler Room

Originally, the ground floor of the north wing as built by Joseph Potter in 1805–9 consisted of the housekeeper's and footmen's rooms, with the Gothick chapel above, on the first floor. In 1935–6 the wing was entirely remodelled by the 6th Marquess of Anglesey, who replaced the chapel by a new range of bedrooms and bathrooms, and formed a long rectangular Dining Room on the ground floor. The chapel had previously been transformed into a theatre by the 5th Marquess (see p.50).

In 1936 Lord Anglesey commissioned Rex Whistler to paint what was to be his last as well as the most extensive of his large murals, more unified and more accomplished than his Tate Gallery work, or his drawing-room at Mottisfont in Hampshire (also NT). Whistler's first conception for the main wall seems to have been entirely different from the completed work – a townscape with figures seen through a colonnade – but

the maritime setting of Plas Newydd, and in particular the views from this room, must have formed in him the notion of reflecting the dramatic mountain landscape of Snowdonia in a vast *capriccio*, which would at the same time embrace architecture, ships and the sea.

The bones of the composition were sketched on to the bare plaster of the long wall before the artist began work on the giant canvas, woven in France in one piece 58 feet long, whose arrival in London, the artist wrote to his patron, caused 'great amazement & interest in canvas & jute circles!' As a prominent stage designer, Whistler was able to secure the use of a theatre workshop in Lambeth where the great canvas could be raised and lowered in relation to the platform from which he worked. When it was largely completed, in June 1937, it was taken down to Plas Newydd and glued to the

(*Right*)
Rex Whistler's self-portrait from the Rex Whistler Room mural

(*Left*)
Detail from the mural in the Rex Whistler Room

plaster. Whistler himself came in August and reworked some passages, while supervising the decoration he had devised for the rest of the room with its gilded cornice, painted coffering in the ceiling and trophies in grisaille over the chimney-pieces (inscribed with the Christian names of the 6th Marquess and his wife).

Much of the composition is purely imaginary, but there are numerous architectural and personal references. Of the former, the steeple of St Martin-in-the-Fields, Trajan's Column, the Round Tower at Windsor and the Roman church of S. Nome di Maria can be seen, the Italian buildings perhaps recalled from Whistler's time at the British School in Rome. The family appears in many guises: on the triumphal arch on the left is an inscription in 'dog-Latin' commemorating the 'founding of the city' by the Marquess, and his equestrian statue stands in front of it; at the far end in the 'gallery' (reminiscent of the Palladian bridge at Wilton) can be seen two French bulldogs and a pug, which belonged to Lady Anglesey's daughters, as well as her book and spectacles. The 'baby' cello belonged to the 7th Marquess as a boy.

In the centre of the main wall Lord and Lady Anglesey's arms are shown as if carved in stone on the ends of the parapet wall, and here too are Neptune's trident and crown carelessly propped up against an urn, and wet footprints leading up the steps from the sea – as if to suggest that the sea-god himself had joined the family at the dinner table.

Almost by way of a signature, Whistler added in the arcade at the other end the figure of a young man sweeping up leaves – this is a self-portrait, the last one before his death in action only a few years later.

Silver

On the dining-table is a silver-gilt trophy made by Whistler's ancestor Paul Storr and presented to the 1st Marquess by the Prince Regent, the Duke of Cumberland, and the officers of the Hussar Brigade which he commanded in the Peninsula in 1808, in recognition of the 'Courage and Talent' he displayed in that command.

Architectural Drawings

In a small room beyond are grouped many of the original drawings for the house, including James Wyatt's designs for the Saloon and Ante-Room, of 1795, and Joseph Potter's of about the same date for the Gothick Hall and Music Room, and for the Chapel built in 1805–9. A watercolour of the east front by Moses Griffith, dated 1776, is of particular interest in showing parts of the original house and the extent of Sir Nicholas Bayly's mid-eighteenth-century gothicisation of it; two other drawings by the same artist, of the east and west fronts in 1806, in turn show the results of Wyatt and Potter's various alterations in the 1790s.

The Cavalry Museum

Occupying several of the former 'domestic offices' is a permanent exhibition of relics and pictures of the 1st Marquess, and of his part in the Battle of Waterloo, which is graphically portrayed in Denis Dighton's epic painting of the action. The picture is of great interest to military historians for its accurate depiction of the uniforms: it even shows some of the shakoes and sabretaches with their oilskin protective covers on. (The eve of the battle had been wet.)

There are several more likenesses of the Marquess himself, including a marble bust by James Sherwood Westmacott (1823–88?), a spirited equestrian portrait signed by R. T. Bott (fl.1847–62), and a painting by Constantine Fidelio Coene (1780–1841) of a fictitious meeting between Wellington and Uxbridge shortly after the cavalry commander's right leg had been amputated. This painting was a gift from the descendant of one of the sitters, the 7th Duke of Wellington, to his godson, the present Earl of

The Anglesey Leg
(Cavalry Museum)

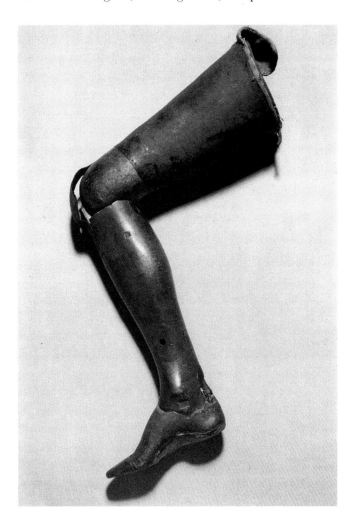

49

Uxbridge, a descendant of the other. Lord Uxbridge later generously presented the painting to the National Trust.

Other reminders of Lord Anglesey's dreadful injury on that day include a sprig of willow from the tree near the scene of the injury, in whose shade the limb was buried with military honours, and the leather 'stump cap' worn subsequently by Lord Anglesey. Finally, there is an example of one of the Marquess's artificial limbs, designed by James Potts of Northumberland, and of a type still known as 'the Anglesey leg', the world's first articulated wooden leg.

Among the exhibits are medals and orders, including the 1st Marquess of Anglesey's Garter and Order of the Bath. In the corridor, there are medals awarded to his son, General Lord George Paget, second-in-command of the cavalry under Lord Cardigan at Balaclava during the Crimean War (1854–6). His coolness under fire was such that he smoked a cigar throughout the Charge of the Light Brigade.

In the next room to the right of the corridor is exhibited the collection of uniforms given to the National Trust by Lt-Col E. N. Ryan, MD, TD. Colonel Ryan, of the Royal Army Medical Corps, formed the major part of his collection of military uniforms during the First World War. Colonel Ryan's international approach to collecting was unusual at the time, and his collection provides a rare opportunity to compare the cavalry uniforms of different countries.

Military prints connected with Lord Anglesey's campaigns and the regiments with which he served, as well as others concerned more generally with the British cavalry, hang in the corridor. There are also some interesting drawings of Lord Anglesey in old age and a particularly fine set of four watercolours of military uniforms by W. Heath, 1822.

The Dancing Marquess

In the corridor at the end of the tour is a selection of photographs of the 5th Marquess of Anglesey, as he appeared at the 'Gaiety Theatre' which he installed in what was the chapel at Plas Newydd (then renamed Anglesey Castle).

These productions were distinguished above all by lavish expenditure on the Marquess's wardrobe, and, despite the assistance of some leading professional actors, seldom rose above the level of pantomime. Lord Anglesey invariably took centre-stage, performing his 'Butterfly Dance' to rapturous applause on many occasions; among the many surviving contemporary notices ('. . . his Lordship makes a decided hit in the song "Ping Pong". . .'), one report explains the true appeal of these spectacles in remarking of his performance as 'Pekoe' in *Aladdin* that the Marquess, 'though the lines he has to speak may not be of the highest brilliancy, wears a costume that may be worth anything from £100,000 upwards'.

In one production, performed in 1902, the Marquess appears to have made an early essay in 'kitchen sink drama'. His portrayal of penury and domestic hardship in *Daily*

The 5th Marquess converted the Plas Newydd chapel into a theatre

Life ('. . . hardly equal, as a piece of stagecraft, to his lordship's adaptation of "*At the Telephone*". . .') must have seemed ironic even to an audience unaware of the devastating effects the Marquess's activities were to have on the Paget inheritance.

Aside from the theatre, the 5th Marquess expressed his extravagant tastes in historical balls and firework displays (for his birthday in 1903 these included 'Batteries of Jewelled Headed Cobras', 'Ascent of Monster Balloons' and 'Salvo of Golden Saucissons' as preludes to a 'Grand Presentation of the Facade of Anglesey Castle'), and in the fitting out of his own apartments with mauve velvet and filigree gold ornaments. Meanwhile in the kennels he kept 'such numbers of terriers and pugs, Pomeranians, collies, chows, St Bernards and huge Borzois that you begin to fancy you have strayed into a Crystal Palace dog show'.

He died in retreat from his creditors at Monte Carlo at the age of 30 in 1905. Some years later, when his successor, his cousin the 6th Marquess, was forced to consider selling the family's principal seat, a newspaper expressed the opinion that 'It seems melancholy that so much connected with the past of an ancient house should all have to be sacrificed to a reckless prodigal's contemptible follies'.

The Garden*

The damp atmosphere and low susceptibility to frost of the maritime situation make the Menai coast of Anglesey an ideal habitat for exotics and shrubs, exploited at Baron Hill near Beaumaris in the eighteenth century and at Rhianfa near Menai Bridge in the nineteenth, and in our own century above all at Plas Newydd. The soils of the Plas Newydd grounds are highly various in quality, acidity and depth, making for variety in the plantings that have become established over two hundred years within the late eighteenth-century framework.

Little is known of the character of the garden before that time, when Lord Uxbridge began work in a spirit of modest and amateur 'improvement' with the help of his friend and neighbour Col Peacock of Plas Llanfair. There was new planting in 1792, but in the opinion of Humphry Repton, writing in his report seven years later, 'they have proceeded too hastily at Plas Newydd in grubbing hedges and pulling down cottages, for the sake of clearing an extent of open lawn in a direction where plantations ought to be encouraged to screen a bleak country'. It was a common mistake, he wrote, to confuse mere extensiveness with beauty.

Many of Repton's 'hints for the improvement of the place' therefore stemmed from the conviction that more should be made of the woods that embraced the house on the inland side. New plantings would be essential, but where possible he advised the retention of relic trees, which should be surrounded with young brushwood. Since the illustrations are missing from Repton's 'Red Book', his detailed recommendations are not always clear, but comparison of the estate plans of 1798 and 1804 shows that most of his broad principles were put into effect. Survivors of his plantings include most notably the groups of beeches at the top of the stepped path to the house and a little way to the south-west, some grand sycamores and a group of limes of a rare form along the sea walk to the south.

The 1st Marquess undertook further large-scale tree-planting after 1815, but, as with the house, there followed a period of little or no activity. Indeed, Louisa Stuart Costello's account of Plas Newydd in 1845 refers to '. . . the entire neglect into which it has fallen for more than twenty years'.

The 5th, or 'Dancing', Marquess was probably the next to make any significant changes, notably the addition of a conservatory to the north and in line with the house, below which he laid out a series of elaborate beds. In the 1920s his cousin

* A separate guide to the garden, with a plan and more details of plant names, can be purchased in the shop or at the house.

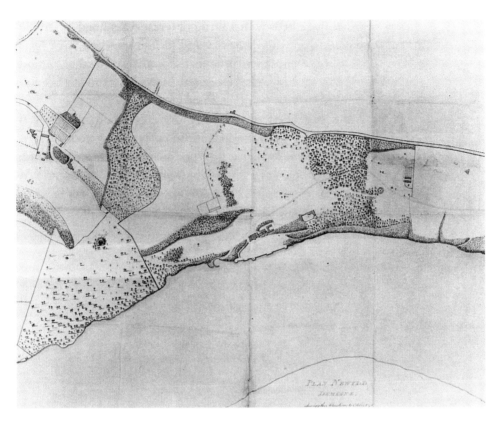

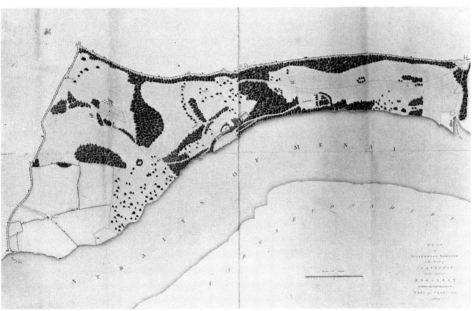

(*Top*) Plan of the Plas Newydd Demesne in 1798　(*Bottom*) Plan of the Demesne in 1804

the 6th Marquess replaced these beds with a series of terraces retained by rubble walls and planted in an Italianate style with cypresses and formal standard bays, ornamented with statuary. This terrace garden is now in the course of further remodelling by the National Trust in partnership with the present Marquess, who has been responsible for many other significant improvements since his succession in 1947.

The following year the 2nd Lord Aberconway presented Lord Anglesey with a quantity of 'thinnings' from the famous rhododendron collection at Bodnant as a wedding present, and encouraged him to revive the rhododendron garden which the 6th Marquess had established in the 1930s, but which had declined during the Second World War. On the advice of the 11th Lord Digby, the garden has been formed beneath a large stand of Scots pine, Douglas fir and oak approximately three-quarters of a mile from the house.

For three years from 1948 a consignment of Bodnant plants arrived at Plas Newydd in the care of two gardeners 'equipped', as Lord Anglesey recalls, 'with shiningly polished spades to plant them'. Many of these were the famous Bodnant hybrids from *R. griersonianum*, which greatly enriched the original plantings of *R. fortunei*, *R. praevernum*,

The rhododendron garden

PAVILLION & GREEN HOUSE FOR A GOTHIC MANSION.

Repton proposed building a Gothick conservatory against the south-east corner of the Octagon Room. The idea was never adopted, but this engraving of the scheme was published in Repton's *Theory and Practice of Landscape Gardening* in 1803

R. falconeri, *R. williamsianum* and others. The garden is reached by the long walk from the east (seaward) side of the house.

At the other end of the walk is the entrance to the extensive pleasure ground known by the family (for what reason is now forgotten) as the West Indies. Bordering the wide lawns are beds of massed hydrangeas, camellias (some of which came from the conservatory at Beaudesert as long ago as 1914), azaleas, Japanese maples and cherries, with many specimen conifers including the Blue Atlantic Cedar. Above this area, the National Trust and Lord Anglesey have replaced an exhausted orchard with an Australasian arboretum, planted in the early 1980s with a selection of eucalyptus and a collection of Nothofagus or Southern Beech, chosen with the advice of the late Earl of Bradford.

At its southern extremity the garden is closed by a double avenue of yew and macrocarpa cypresses, on the line of the eighteenth-century ha-ha, which, though no longer complete, runs intermittently round the inland edge of the garden.

The Bayly and Paget Families

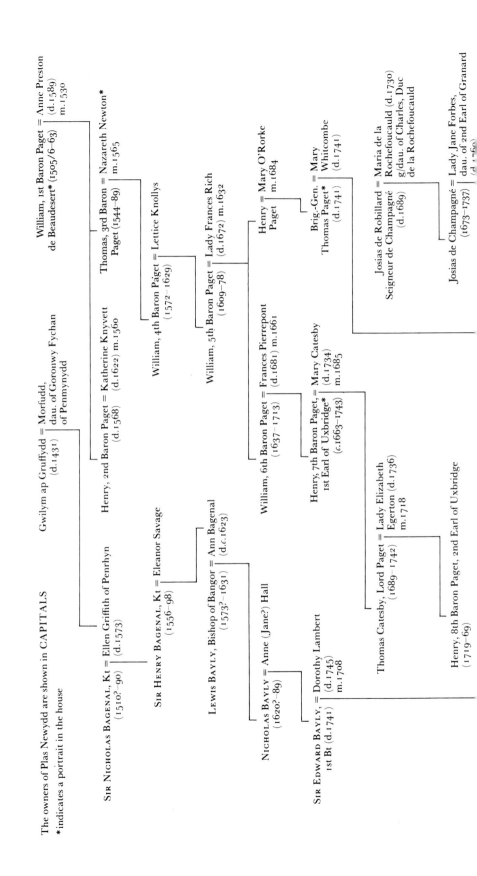

The owners of Plas Newydd are shown in CAPITALS
*indicates a portrait in the house

Gwilym ap Gruffydd = Morfudd,
(d.1431)   dau. of Goronwy Fychan
of Penmynydd

William, 1st Baron Paget = Anne Preston
de Beaudesert* (1505/6–63)   (d.1589)
m.1530

Thomas, 3rd Baron = Nazareth Newton*
Paget (1544–89)   m.1565

William, 4th Baron Paget = Lettice Knollys
(1572–1629)

William, 5th Baron Paget = Lady Frances Rich
(1609–78)   (d.1672) m.1632

Henry = Mary O'Rorke
Paget   m.1684

Brig.-Gen. = Mary
Thomas Paget*   Whitcombe
(d.1741)   (d.1741)

Josias de Robillard = Maria de la
Seigneur de Champagné   Rochefoucauld (d.1730)
(d.1689)   g/dau. of Charles, Duc
de la Rochefoucauld

Josias de Champagné = Lady Jane Forbes,
(1673–1737)   dau. of 2nd Earl of Granard

SIR NICHOLAS BAGENAL, Kt = Ellen Griffith of Penrhyn
(1510?–90)   (d.1573)

SIR HENRY BAGENAL, Kt = Eleanor Savage
(1556–98)

Henry, 2nd Baron Paget = Katherine Knyvett
(d.1568)   (d.1622) m.1560

LEWIS BAYLY, Bishop of Bangor = Ann Bagenal
(1573?–1631)   (d.c.1623)

William, 6th Baron Paget = Frances Pierrepont
(1637–1713)   (d.1681) m.1661

NICHOLAS BAYLY = Anne (Jane?) Hall
(1620?–89)

Henry, 7th Baron Paget, = Mary Catesby
1st Earl of Uxbridge*   (d.1734)
(c.1663–1743)   m.1685

SIR EDWARD BAYLY, = Dorothy Lambert
1st Bt (d.1741)   (d.1745)
m.1708

Thomas Catesby, Lord Paget = Lady Elizabeth
(1689–1742)   Egerton (d.1736)
m.1718

Henry, 8th Baron Paget, 2nd Earl of Uxbridge
(1719–69)

Arthur Champagné, Dean of Clanmacnoise (1714–1800) = Marianne Hamon (d.1784)

Sir Nicholas Bayly, 2nd Bt* (1709–82) = Caroline Paget* (d.1766) m.1737

Henry Bayly, 9th Baron Paget of Beaudesert, 1st Earl of Uxbridge* (2nd creation 1784) (1744–1812) = Jane Champagné (1746–1817) m.1767

Lady Caroline (1) = Henry William, = (2) Lady Charlotte Wellesley (née Cadogan) (1781–1853) m.1810
Villiers* (1774–1835) m.1795 divorced 1810
created 1st Marquess of Anglesey 1815* (1768–1854)

Sir Arthur* (1771–1840) = Lady Augusta Boringdon (née Fane)

Caroline* (1773–1847) = Hon. John Capel

Sir Edward* (1775–1849) = (1) Frances Bagot (2) Lady Harriet Legge

Jane* (1798–1876) = Francis, 2nd Marquess Conyngham

Sir Charles (1778–1839) = Elizabeth Monk

3 other sons; 4 other daughters

Caroline* (1796–1874) = Charles, 5th Duke of Richmond (1791–1860)

Henry, = (1) Eleanora Campbell (1799–1828) m.1820 = (2) Henrietta Bagot* (1815–44) m.1833 = (3) Ellen Burnaud (d.1874) m.1860
2nd Marquess of Anglesey* (1797–1869)

2 other sons and 3 daus.

6 sons and 4 daus.

Alexander (1839–96) = Hon. Hester Stapleton-Cotton (d.1930) m.1880

Henry, 3rd Marquess of Anglesey (1821–80)

Henry, 4th Marquess of Anglesey (1835–98) = (2) Blanche Curwen (d.1877) m.1874

Charles, 6th Marquess of Anglesey,* = Lady Marjorie Manners,* dau. of 8th Duke of Rutland (1883–1946) m.1912
Anglesey* (1885–1947)

Henry, 5th Marquess of Anglesey (1875–1905)

Henry, = Shirley, dau. of Charles Morgan m.1948
7th Marquess of Anglesey* (b.1922)

Katharine = (1) Lt-Col Jocelyn Gurney = (2) Charles Farrell

Amelia (b.1963) = Andrew Singleton

Isabella (b.1990)

Henry (b.1994)

Caroline* (1913–76) = Sir Michael Duff, Bt

Elizabeth (b.1916) = Raimund von Hofmannsthal

Mary (b.1918)

Rose (b.1919) = Hon. John McLaren

Henrietta (b.1949) = Timothy Megarry

Alexander, Earl of Uxbridge (b.1950) = Georgina Young

Sophia (b.1954) = Robert Keir

Rupert (b.1957) = Louise Youngman

Katherine (b.1981)

Matthew (b.1985)

Benedict (b.1986)

Clara (b.1988)

Samuel (b.1986)

Oliver (b.1987)

Jack (b.1989)

The Griffith, Bayly and Paget Families

Like Penrhyn near Bangor, which was acquired by the National Trust in 1951, Plas Newydd belonged in the fifteenth century to the Griffiths 'of Penrhyn'. Members of this powerful family were the first in North Wales to emerge as the owners of great landed estates. Parts, if not all, of the considerable properties on Anglesey seem to have come to Gwilym ap Gruffydd (d.1431), by his marriage with Morfudd, daughter of Goronwy Fychan of Penmynydd, whose domain lies only a few miles from Plas Newydd. Morfudd's uncle was great-grandfather of Henry VII.

In 1553 the Plas Newydd estate passed to the Bagenal family, when Ellen Griffith (d.1573) married Sir Nicholas Bagenal, Queen Elizabeth's marshal of the army in Ireland. It again changed hands when his granddaughter, Ann (d. *c.*1623) wed Lewis Bayly, Bishop of Bangor. This distinguished divine was the author of *The Practice of Piety*, which enjoyed the widest fame among puritans in the seventeenth and eighteenth centuries, being translated into numerous languages. Bunyan ascribed to its influence the beginning of his spiritual experiences. Bishop Bayly also acted as chaplain to Henry, Prince of Wales, and on his death in 1612, to Charles I. Bishop Bayly's son, Nicholas Bayly 'of Plas Newydd' (1620?–89), was Governor of Galway and the Isles of Arran as well as Gentleman of the Bedchamber to Charles II. His son, Edward (d. 1741), was created a baronet by George II in 1730. Seven years later Edward's son, Sir Nicholas Bayly, married Caroline Paget, uniting two of the region's leading families.

Caroline Paget was great-great-great-great granddaughter of William, 1st Baron Paget de Beaudesert in Staffordshire, one of Henry VIII's 'New Men', a skilful states-man who, unlike so many of his colleagues in Tudor times, died in his bed. She was also, as we shall see, heir to his title and estates. Of William Paget's origins nothing is certain. A Staffordshire historian, unsupported, states that the family were 'nailers, or rather nail factors, who gathered the nails from the forgers and placed them on the market as merchandise'. In the *Visitation of Staffordshire*, 1583, Paget's father is given as 'Pagitt, of London, mediocris fortunae vir'.

Paget's reputation as a trimmer seems to have been justified. His advice to politi-cians, however, is unobjectionable: 'Deliberate maturelye in all things. Execute quyck-elye the Determynations. Do justice without respecte . . . Be affable to the good and sterne to the evill . . . Thus God will prosper youe, the King favour youe and all men love youe.' A protégé of Bishop Stephen Gardiner, he was one of Henry's chief advisers and an executor of his will. From the 1540s onwards, many of the King's more delicate diplomatic negotiations were entrusted to him. The Emperor Charles V is said to have remarked that Paget deserved 'as well to be a king as to represent one', and

William, 1st Baron Paget, the founder of the Paget fortunes; ? Flemish, sixteenth-century (Gothick Hall)

Beaudesert in Staffordshire, the home of William, 1st Baron Paget; by an unknown English artist, *c.*1810 (Middle Landing)

in comparing the three English ambassadors who had been sent to him from time to time, declared that Wolsey had promised much and done nothing, Morrisson had promised and done much, while Paget had promised nothing and done all.

Paget is credited with the following axioms: 'Fly the courte, Speke little, Care less, Desire nothing, Never earnest; In answer cold, Learne to spare, Spend in measure, Care for home, Pray often, Live better, And Dye well.' It was said of him that 'his education was better than his birth; his knowledge higher than his education; his parts above his knowledge, and his experience above his parts.'

Henry VIII appointed Paget as one of the guardians of his young son, and during Edward VI's reign he was a supporter of 'Protector' Somerset. In 1549, two years after Edward's accession, Somerset's enemies produced evidence to show that Paget's accounts as Chancellor of the Duchy of Lancaster were corrupt. He was arrested and deprived of his honours. These included the Garter, his grant of arms, his lands and his goods. His low birth was the chief reason given for degrading him from the Garter, it being said that 'he was no gentleman of bloud, neither of father's side nor mother's side'. On the death of Edward in 1553, he joined Lady Jane Grey's council, possibly under constraint, for he was one of those who sanctioned the proclamation of Mary as Queen. With Mary and her husband, Philip II of Spain, he was for most of their reign in high favour, being made Lord Privy Seal in 1555 and employed once more upon foreign missions.

On the accession of Elizabeth I in 1558, Paget retired. Five years later he died, possessed of considerable fortune and extensive estates. Chief of these was Beaudesert in Staffordshire, which had been granted him by Henry VIII. The great house he built there, much added to in the early nineteenth century and again just before World War I, was pulled down in the 1930s. It was put on the market in 1924, but it was not until ten years later that it was bought by house-breakers. Bricks from Beaudesert were used in the re-facing of the almost contemporary St James's Palace, which was decaying as a result of centuries of London's pollution. Amongst the other church lands which Paget obtained after the Dissolution of the Monasteries were estates at West Drayton and Uxbridge and the Benedictine Abbey of Burton in Staffordshire, which also owned properties in Derbyshire, Warwickshire, Leicestershire and Cheshire.

Three of his sons, including the 2nd and the 3rd Barons (who partly rebuilt Beaudesert), were Roman Catholic exiles and conspirators. By contrast the 4th Baron, son of the 3rd, was a staunch Protestant who served with the Earl of Essex at the taking of Cadiz in 1596. He became a Commissioner for Virginia and was an original member of the Bermudas Company for the plantation of the Somers Islands, where a fort and a tribe were named after him. He was also a member of the Council of the Amazon River Company. He died in 1629.

In 1640 his son, William, the 5th Baron, voted against King Charles in the Lords, and was one of those who petitioned him to summon a parliament for the redress of grievances. It was only when he realised that Parliament actually intended to resort to arms that he joined the King. He raised a regiment for him which did good service at Edgehill. After the King's execution his estates were sequestered by the Commonwealth, and he was fined £1,000. At the Restoration his petitions to make good his losses were not attended to. A seventeenth-century writer described his character thus, 'Noe parts that I know of except a good stomack.'

His eldest son, another William, the 6th Baron, was a distinguished diplomat, first in Vienna, and then, from 1693, as ambassador-extraordinary to Turkey, where his prudent negotiations resulted in the Treaty of Carlowitz (1699). He was much liked by the Sultan of Turkey, who personally persuaded William III to keep him on at his Court, and who loaded him with presents when he eventually left for home in 1702. Of these he presented twelve superb Turkish horses to Queen Anne. He undertook a number of other special diplomatic missions before he died in 1713.

The 6th Baron's son, Henry, MP for Staffordshire for sixteen years, a Lord of the Treasury and Captain of the Yeomen of the Guard, was created Earl of Uxbridge in 1714, soon after his appointment as Envoy Extraordinary to the Elector of Hanover, who later that year came to England as George I. Thomas Catesby Paget, Uxbridge's son, who died before him, was a Gentleman of the Bedchamber to George II and an amateur poet and writer, whose works 'were compos'd for the Noble Author's own

Amusement in the Country, during the intervals of bad weather, in Hunting-seasons'. They so closely imitated Pope's that Paget was thought for some time to have been the author of the anonymous 'Essay on Man'. His son Henry became the 8th Baron, second and last Earl of Uxbridge of the first creation. Reputed to have an inordinate love of money, this unrenowned gentleman died unmarried and intestate in 1769.

The 1st Baron (Henry VIII's secretary of state), to make sure of the succession, had contrived that his peerage, created in 1549, should be transmittable through the female line in the event of the male line dying out. With the 8th Baron's death, this happened – 220 years later. The female link through which the barony was passed

Caroline Paget, Lady Bayly; by
Enoch Seeman (Staircase Hall)

on was that Caroline Paget who, as has been shown, married Sir Nicholas Bayly. Caroline in fact died three years before the 8th Baron, but her son, Henry Bayly, duly became the 9th Baron at the age of 25.

This slightly eccentric, unambitious man, who became 1st Earl of Uxbridge of the second creation when the earldom was revived for him in 1784, succeeded to a splendid heritage. Eleven years after his first accession of rank and wealth, the new Baron found himself master of a second fortune. In 1752 a wealthy West Country landowner by the name of Peter Walter made a will which proved that in the event of his own line failing, all his possessions should pass to the heir of Sir Nicholas Bayly. Why he should have done so remains a mystery to this day. Nevertheless the strange terms of this will were put into effect in 1780, and extensive lands in Dorset and Somerset came into Henry Bayly Paget's hands.

On his father's death two years later he succeeded to the Bayly properties in Ireland and North Wales, including, of course, Plas Newydd. The total territory which now was his added up to some 100,000 acres. Under much of it lay vast mineral wealth:

Henry Bayly, 1st Earl of Uxbridge; by George Romney (Music Room)

coal in Staffordshire and copper in the famous Parys and Mona mines at Amlwch.

Uxbridge, as his portraits show, justified 'Peter Pindar's' couplet:

> And he who lours as if he meant to bite
> Is Earl of Uxbridge with his face of night.

His 'louring' looks and swarthy hue belied his character. All the vast opportunities which came his way failed to fire him with personal ambition. His outstanding characteristics (if so positive a term can be applied to so negative a man) were his lack of personal aspirations and his love of ease, though on occasion he could sacrifice both for the advancement of his sons' careers. He had, besides, a reputation for whimsy and a dry sense of humour, both of which, no less than his disinclination for business and for letter-writing, sorely tried his family and friends. There is a story handed down in the family which well illustrates his brand of humour. On one occasion, it is said, a son of the house took leave of his father at Beaudesert and rode off to London. After some hours of fast riding he was overtaken by a groom, who asked him to return home at once upon urgent business. Galloping back as fast as he could, he entered his father's room – to be met with: 'Oh, my boy, you forgot to close my door.'

Lord Uxbridge's loyalty to his sovereign was unswerving. George III never had a more constant and unquestionable parliamentary supporter, for Uxbridge saw to it that the House of Commons seats in his gift were filled by relations and friends in steady support of the Tories. His personal friendship with the King, and Lady Uxbridge's with Queen Charlotte, were close: the stationing of Uxbridge's regiment of militia at Windsor over many years brought them into frequent contact. A further tie was a mutual love of music. This, in Uxbridge's case, led him on occasions to patronise promising young musicians, and to set them up in their careers. Among those he befriended was the composer and organist George Baker, who in his seventeenth year left his parents in Exeter to try to make a musical living in London. So as to attract attention, it is said, and being short of money with which to buy instruments, he collected a quantity of horseshoes of varying sizes and strung them across the street. One day Lord Uxbridge, who happened to be passing, heard him playing upon them and was so entranced by the boy's ingenuity and skill that he there and then took him into his household and arranged for his musical training.

It was Uxbridge who, continuing the process begun by Sir Nicholas Bayly, refashioned Plas Newydd, changing the house from a medieval manor into an eighteenth-century Gothick mansion worthy of a rich nobleman, a process more or less completed by the time of his death in 1812, when he was succeeded by his eldest son and heir, Field Marshal Henry William (Bayly) Paget, 2nd Earl of Uxbridge and 1st Marquess of Anglesey.

This remarkable soldier-statesman was born in 1768. He was considered 'le plus beau garçon d'Angleterre' and never lost his striking looks. In 1816 Baron Stockmar described him thus: 'A tall, well-made man; wild, martial face, high forehead, with

Henry, Lord Paget, later 1st Marquess of Anglesey, as Lieut.-Colonel of the 7th Light Dragoons; by John Hoppner and Sawrey Gilpin, exh. RA, 1798 (Music Room)

a large hawk's nose, which makes a small, deep angle where it joins the forehead. A great deal of ease in his manners.' At 22 he entered Parliament. At 25 he raised the 80th Regiment of Foot and in 1794 fought with it (and later as a brigade commander) in Flanders under the 'noble Duke of York'. Three years later he became Lieutenant-Colonel of the 7th Light Dragoons (later Hussars). Under his command the regiment became one of the finest cavalry units in the army. His first actions were fought in the Netherlands in 1799. By the time he went to Portugal in 1808, he had become a lieutenant-general. Taking command of Sir John Moore's small cavalry force in that year, he achieved brilliant successes against vastly more numerous French cavalry, being largely responsible for screening Moore's famous retreat to Corunna.

After that he saw no further service in the Peninsula, partly because he was senior to Wellington, and partly because of his celebrated elopement with the Duke's sister-in-law. As he wrote to his brother Charles in the spring of 1809, 'An attachment is unfortunately formed between us. It is fought against for a long time. Alas, not long enough – passion gets the better of reason and finally we are driven to the necessity of the present step.' By his first wife, Caroline Villiers, daughter of the 4th Earl of Jersey, he had eight children. By his second, Charlotte Wellesley (née Cadogan), whom he married in 1810 after costly divorce proceedings, he sired a further ten.

After Napoleon's escape from Elba in 1815, Uxbridge was appointed commander of the Allied cavalry in the Netherlands (second-in-command to Wellington). His retreat through Genappe on 17 June, and his brilliant, if impetuous, handling of the cavalry at the Battle of Waterloo the following day, earned him lasting renown. His right leg was smashed by grapeshot as he was riding off the field with the Duke at the end of the day. Looking down at his shattered limb, he is supposed to have exclaimed: 'By God, sir, I've lost my leg!' To which the Duke, momentarily removing the spy-glass from his eye, replied: 'By God, sir, so you have!' – at once resuming his scrutiny of the retreating French. Within three weeks of the amputation of his limb, he was back in London. The Prince Regent (later George IV) at once made him a Marquess, declaring 'that he *loved* him . . . and that he was his best officer and his best subject'.

Some years later Anglesey was provided with an early example of the recently invented articulated wooden leg. The same type, known as 'the Anglesey leg', was still being commercially advertised as late as 1914. One of those worn by Anglesey is maintained in working condition at Plas Newydd.

In 1827 Anglesey became Master-General of the Ordnance under Canning, and in 1828 Lord Lieutenant of Ireland under Wellington. Relieved the following year because of his advocacy of Catholic Emancipation, he went for a second time to Dublin in 1830 under Lord Grey's Whig administration, retiring from ill-health in 1833. Thirteen years later, in Lord John Russell's government, he once more became Master-General. He finally relinquished office only when the government fell, not because he was then 84 years of age. Two years later he died.

Since his father had twice modernised Plas Newydd and he seldom lived there himself, it is not surprising that the 1st Marquess made almost no architectural or decorative impact on the house. That he had a taste for modern décor is, however, clear from the commissions he gave to the firm of Gillow, for furnishings and decorative work at Beaudesert, and at Uxbridge House in London.

In 1860 the column, which had been erected in 1817 within sight of Plas Newydd by the inhabitants of Anglesey and Caernarfon 'in grateful commemoration of the distinguished military achievements of their countryman', was crowned with 'a colossal statue' of him in bronze.

Three of the Marquess's brothers gained distinction. Sir Arthur Paget was a noted diplomat. General Sir Edward Paget lost an arm when second-in-command to Wellington in Spain and became Commander-in-Chief in India. Vice-Admiral Sir

A sketch of the 1st Marquess of Anglesey in old age; by Sylvia Doyle (Cavalry Museum)

Charles Paget made a name for himself in a number of naval engagements during the Napoleonic wars.

The 1st Marquess's eighteen children presented him with 73 grandchildren. None of these nor their descendants can lay claim to any great celebrity. Large numbers of them married into other noble families. They were for the most part good examples of the 'idle rich'. Lord Melbourne is supposed, when urged to do something about national education, to have countered with: 'What is all this nonsense about education? The Pagets have got on well enough without it!'

The 2nd Marquess, a *roué*, was for a time Lord Chamberlain to Queen Victoria and is reputed to have kept his mistress as housekeeper in Buckingham Palace. His brother, Lord Alfred Paget, served the Queen for 30 years, first as equerry and later as Clerk-Marshal of the Royal Household. He and the young Queen are said to have been in love, each of them keeping a miniature of the other around the necks of their respective dogs. Soon after the Queen's accession in 1837 there were thirteen male and female members of the Paget family holding jobs at Court, all of them good Whigs, mostly appointed by Melbourne. In 1841 Prince Albert swept most of these courtiers away, allegedly describing them as a 'plague of locusts'.

(*Left*) From left to right: the Earl of Uxbridge (later the 5th Marquess); Lord Berkeley Paget; the 4th Marquess; and Lord Alexander Paget. The photograph was taken in 1896.

(*Right*) The 5th Marquess in costume

The 3rd Marquess, MP for South Staffordshire for a short period, died without issue in 1880 and was succeeded by his half-brother, the 4th Marquess, who was a truly whimsical man. Not liking the smell of hounds, he is said to have had those of the Anglesey Hunt sprayed with perfume. Glorying in the title Vice-Admiral of North Wales, he kept his yacht moored off Plas Newydd. It is believed that he used to have steam kept up whenever he was in residence, just in case he wished to go for a sail. More often than not, the legend goes, he would have himself and his guests rowed aboard, address the captain with a cheerful 'All correct, captain?', to be answered by a salute and 'Aye, aye, m'lord'. A sumptuous luncheon would then be served aboard and when it was over everyone would be rowed ashore again.

Lord Alexander Paget, the 4th Marquess's younger brother and the father of the 6th Marquess, was known in the family as 'Uncle Dandy'. Being a younger son, he was comparatively badly off. Reflecting his order of priorities, his wife and children, it was asserted, used to travel by train third-class, his valet second-class and himself first-class. His only other claim to fame was his honorary lieutenancy in the Royal Naval Artillery Volunteers, Liverpool Brigade.

The 4th Marquess had three wives, by the second of whom he was said to have been the father of the 5th Marquess. It is sometimes supposed that the real father was the French actor Benoît Coquelin, though this may be doubted since the eccentrici-

(*Left*) Charles, 6th Marquess of Anglesey; by Rex Whistler, *c.*1937 (Gothick Hall Gallery)
(*Right*) Henry, 7th Marquess of Anglesey in his study

ties of his acknowledged father were at least as pronounced in him. Certainly 'Toppy', as he was known to his friends, lost his mother when only two years old and was brought up in France by Madame Coquelin. From an early age he was fascinated by the theatre and in 1901 he founded his own company, staging lavish productions in the theatre at Plas Newydd which he had converted from the private chapel, supported by prominent actors and actresses from London. Admission was free and neighbours of all classes attended. He toured in the English provinces and is said to have performed his famous 'Butterfly Dance' in Berlin and to have received £100 a week for doing so, every penny of which went to local charities. There is a story that in winter he had braziers kept alight at intervals along the woodland paths at Plas Newydd in case he should wish to warm himself whilst out walking. He is said, on one occasion, to have thrown a £3,000 bejewelled fur coat into one of these braziers because it was making him too hot.

Though very rich, his income exceeding £110,000 a year, the 5th Marquess indulged his passion for jewellery, objects of vertu and clothes to such an extent that the inevitable financial crash came in 1904. This led to what the papers called the 'great Anglesey sales'. These covered no fewer than forty days. The 17,000 lots disposed of ranged from pedigree dogs to motor cars. The jewellery alone fetched £32,819. Up to his death the following year, just short of thirty years of age, his creditors were receiving 6s in the £. The 6th Marquess over the years compensated the local tradesmen – if not Cartiers!

The 6th Marquess, who died in 1947, was the 5th's first cousin. For 22 years he served as Lord Chamberlain to Queen Mary. His wife, Lady Marjorie Manners, daughter of the 8th Duke of Rutland, and sister of Lady Diana Cooper, was, like her mother, an able amateur artist. In the 1930s the 6th Marquess effected the first extensive alterations to Plas Newydd since the early 1800s, making it into one of the most comfortable country houses in Britain. He believed amongst other things that 'every bathroom should have a bedroom', and practised what he preached. It was he who commissioned Rex Whistler's famous dining-room wall paintings.

His only son, the 7th Marquess, a military historian, has been President of the National Museum of Wales, Chairman of the Historic Buildings Council for Wales and a founder member of the National Heritage Memorial Fund. Plas Newydd and 169 acres of surrounding land, including one and a half miles of the Menai Strait coastline, were given to the National Trust by the 7th Marquess in 1976.

The present Marchioness of Anglesey, daughter of Charles Morgan, the novelist, playwright and essayist, has been Chairman of the National Federation of Women's Institutes, of the Welsh Arts Council and of the Broadcasting Complaints Commission. She was appointed DBE in 1983. She and the Marquess still live in a part of Plas Newydd, thus continuing his family's connection with the house which has lasted for over five centuries.

Short Bibliography

The great majority of the family papers are deposited in the library of the University College of North Wales, Bangor; others are still at Plas Newydd. Repton's 'Red Book' of 1799 is in the National Library of Wales, Aberystwyth. Drawings for Plas Newydd by James Wyatt and Joseph Potter are in the RIBA Library, London, and in the collection of Potter's son, now in Sheffield City Library.

Anglesey, Marquess of, *The Capel Letters 1814–1817*, London, 1955.

Anglesey, Marquess of, *One-Leg: The Life and Letters of the First Marquess of Anglesey 1768–1854*, London, 1961.

Anglesey, Marquess of, 'The Garden at Plas Newydd', *Anglesey Antiquarian Society and Field Club Transactions*, 1991.

Blyth, Henry, *The Pocket Venus*, London, 1966.

Hussey, Christopher, 'Plas Newydd', *Country Life*, 24 November and 1 December 1955.

Jackson-Stops, Gervase, 'Plas Newydd', *Country Life*, 24 June and 1 July 1976; 'Exotics in a Repton Landscape', *Country Life*, 4 August 1977.

Jackson-Stops, Gervase, 'Plas Newydd', *Transactions of the Ancient Monuments Society*, vol. xxix, 1985, a volume published in honour of the Marquess of Anglesey which also includes articles on the Menai bridges by Elisabeth Beazley, on Beaudesert by Howard Colvin, on the lost Paget Tomb by Christopher Harrison, and on the Paget family by F. S. Andrus.

Ramage, Helen, *Portraits of an Island: Eighteenth Century Anglesey*, Llangefni, 1987.

Royal Commission on Ancient Monuments in Wales: Anglesey, HMSO, 1937.

Williams, E. A., *Hanes Môn*, 1925, published in a translation by G. Wynne Griffith as *The Day Before Yesterday: Anglesey in the Nineteenth Century*, Llangefni, 1988.

On Rex Whistler

Hussey, Christopher, 'The Rex Whistler Room at Plas Newydd', *Country Life*, 22 February 1946.

Jackson-Stops, Gervase, 'Rex Whistler at Plas Newydd', *Country Life*, 4 August 1977.

Whistler, Laurence, and Ronald Fuller, *The Work of Rex Whistler*, London, 1969.

Whistler, Laurence, *The Laughter and the Urn: The Life of Rex Whistler*, London, 1985.